Historic Gardens of
Mount Holly

Historic Gardens of
Mount Holly
A Legacy of the Landscape

2009

Happy Gardening~

Alicia

A L I C I A   M C S H U L K I S

Charleston · London

THE
History
PRESS

Published by The History Press
Charleston, SC 29403
www.historypress.net

First published 2008

Manufactured in the United States

ISBN 978.1.59629.407.3

Library of Congress Cataloging-in-Publication Data

McShulkis, Alicia.
Historic gardens of Mt. Holly : a legacy of the landscape / Alicia McShulkis.
p. cm.
Includes bibliographical references.
ISBN 978-1-59629-407-3
1. Historic gardens--New Jersey--Mount Holly. 2. Landscape gardening--New Jersey-
-Mount Holly--History. 3. Gardening--New Jersey--Mount Holly--History. 4. Historic
buildings--New Jersey--Mount Holly. 5. Dwellings--New Jersey--Mount Holly--History. 6.
Mount Holly (N.J.)--History. 7. Mount Holly (N.J.)--Buildings, structures, etc. 8. Mount
Holly (N.J.)--Biography. I. Title. II. Title: Historic gardens of Mount Holly.
SB466.U65M685 2008
712.09749'61--dc22
                                    2008037227

Contents

Foreword

A callused palm and dirty fingernails precede a green thumb.
—Contemporary American gardener Michael Garofalo

Alicia, how can I make my wisterias bloom? Alicia, what is that tall plant growing in the corner of my yard? Alicia, why do my roses have brown spots on the leaves? How she must tire of her role as a master gardener and the incessant interrogations from plant-challenged folks like me!

Alicia McShulkis, master gardener, purveyor of gardens, history and culture, is known around Mount Holly as one to readily roll up her sleeves and get her hands in the dirt, whether in Mount Holly's public gardens or in coordinating events and promotions for our town. Her ardent efforts in the revitalization of Mount Holly's downtown area, and her contributions to area horticultural and historical societies, have won her formal proclamation from Mount Holly's township council. But it is her success in divulging the beauty of Mount Holly's "secret gardens" and awakening those magnificent beds of floral abundance to local admiration that she may be best known for. Because of this, she is the perfect one to tell their story in *Historic Gardens of Mount Holly*.

In *Historic Gardens of Mount Holly*, Alicia leads you down the garden path and illustrates what seeded the beauty that we proudly display today on our garden tours. Long before our hostas and hydrangeas adorned our porches and pathways, long before our children and pets ran though the hallways of our homes, library and schools, these spectacular gardens and statuesque buildings played a role of necessity for hardworking colonial farmers, of showcase for ornate Victorians and of reverence for the simplistic Quakers. The plot thickens as Alicia introduces unusual plants and gardening practices from the other side of the globe that chanced to assemble in Mount

Holly over the centuries. She shows you how they have naturalized into a horticultural jewel here.

Alicia is a deep admirer of Thomas Jefferson, his music and his gardens of days gone by; she has visited Monticello several times. Through her interest and knowledge of how we evolved as a town and a nation, you will uncover interesting insights that lie behind our history, much like finding a beautifully carved trellis beneath layers of vines. Alicia will unearth facts, like the connections between our third president and some of the gardens and buildings in Mount Holly, the role Mount Holly played in the independence and development of our nation and the works of notable former Mount Holly residents, such as renowned Quaker John Woolman. While a staunch abolitionist and humanitarian, Woolman, like Alicia, was also an avid gardener, and you will learn about his garden and the orchards on his farm, as well as other noteworthy historical gardens kept by Victorian socialites, wealthy immigrants and modest colonials alike.

The history of our gardens is more colorful than a bouquet of zinnias, and if the ribbon that binds the bouquet of flora and history can be thought of as a thread that began in Europe, Asia and Africa that we can trace to our own backyards, then the road to American freedom and the garden paths in Burlington County run side by side. Alicia's admired Jefferson said, "The earth belongs to the living, not the dead." Yet if those who had gone on before us had not calloused their hands and gotten dirt under their fingernails to give us this gift of lasting freedom and eternal beauty, how unremarkable our land, and culture, might be. Instead, with Alicia as our garden tour guide, we see this history bloom vividly before our eyes, urging us to pick up the trowel and cultivate the tradition alongside the gardeners who hoed the rows before us. Perhaps you prefer to just sit back and enjoy the depth of beauty, color and texture we inherited in our gardens in Mount Holly. If so, pour some lemonade and retire to the veranda to begin the adventure as Alicia unveils it.

"There is not a sprig of grass that shoots uninteresting to me," Jefferson said. Remember, behind every seedling is a bit of history; supporting every arbor is somebody's toil. Like Thomas Jefferson and Alicia McShulkis, grow an interest in the story behind what we see and do not take for granted any day. Our landscape did not just evolve overnight without a plan or purpose. In *Historic Gardens of Mount Holly*, there is not a garden tale that will not intrigue you, and you may find yourself inspired to continue the great garden tradition, or start a new one in your own backyard. Alicia will show you how.

Jan Lynn Bastien

Preface

For as long as I can remember, I've been around gardens. My grandparents had one in Kansas, along with their farm. My great-grandma, a Kentucky transplant, had one just down the road from theirs. Every Memorial Day, we'd cut a multitude of flowers—German irises, peonies, lilacs and whatever else happened to be in bloom—and pack up the Buick, heading off to various family members' graves. We'd leave a remembrance on everyone's grave, from Uncle Roger, who died in infancy, to whoever had passed on during the past year. We'd even spare a few flowers to put on someone's grave who didn't seem to have any because we felt bad. (Kids!)

Fast forward, if you will, to present-day Mount Holly, New Jersey, some distance away from the corn and wheat fields of the Midwest. My husband, three kids, three cats, one rabbit and myself moved to Mount Holly eight years ago to a rather large and overgrown, at least for us, Victorian home in need of TLC. For the first time since I had left the Midwest, we had neighbors. Yes, I know we'd had neighbors in the other places we had lived, but these were different. They were interested in what was happening here as we muddled through our many projects.

Many an hour was spent was spent talking to my elderly neighbor, Rosa, over the fence about what was going on here, both in the garden and in the house. She had lived in our house for a time when she first came to the United States. Her garden is much more formal and structured than my free-flowing wildness, complete with plants that like to run away. She passed away a couple of years ago now. I still miss her phone calls telling me I had left the garage door open again.

The one thing about this town that still truly amazes me is its rich gardening history. Once I got on the fast track of learning more about the town, I found it truly phenomenal. Some of America's most noted architects and landscape architects worked here. There's a strong connection to Philadelphia, Mount Holly once being the summer homes of prominent city residents. The Mount Holly Historical Society, especially Eleanor Rich, Gladys Danser and Larry Tigar, have been truly wonderful to me. The Burlington County Lyceum and Mike Eck, the director, have helped with the research immensely.

Without the help from my friend, Barbara Helmechi, whose rendering of the Dunn estate graces the center of this book, we would not be able to get an idea of what it might have looked like. A watercolor she had done several years ago of another garden remnant can also be found in the book. She is a great friend whose support through this whole project is greatly appreciated. She had help from Jessica Caldwell and Walt Ziegler, both local architects.

There are several people I would like to thank for tolerating me through this process. Please bear with me as I go through the list. Thank you to all of the following people: Dennis Rizzo and Jan Bastien, fellow kindred spirits; the Johns family, who were always willing to put up with my erratic schedule and still help with projects; Allan Hollowell, another who was always ready to help out; Jean Messina and Paula Uhland, who kept the names of people to talk to and the research material coming; Joe and Sandy Connor, who probably don't even know they helped out just by caring enough to ask how the book was coming along; my co-workers at Main Street Mount Holly, Lynn Scowcroft, Michelle Watson and Heather McCall, for their moral support and understanding; and Nina Gee, also a former co-worker, for her fantastic photos.

The last people to be thanked are my family: my husband, Joe, who was there to help "talk me down" those times when this all seemed too impossible; my kids, Karine, Joseph and John, along with my parents, who have had to listen to the ravings of someone on the hunt for some small inkling of a fact; my niece, Eleni, who had to put up with me for a week, wondering why "Auntie" was always stopping to smell and photograph the flowers. Bees are good bugs, Eleni! My two cats, Blackie and Wookie, need some recognition. They were the ones that had to listen to the pages being read aloud when I was editing this book. Many a long night was spent with them sitting beside me while I typed away at my computer. I know I probably forgot people, so please accept this "Thank You."

PREFACE

This book only features a few of the gardens located here at one time or another, "but I continue learning." All photos are taken by me unless otherwise noted. Wherever possible, I tried to note if the gardens still existed or not. We are now done with all the preliminaries, so…let's get this started, as the song says.

Gardens of Survival

The Kitchen Garden and the Orchard

Although the popular image of the Native American is a befeathered hunter, it is a startling and salutary fact that 60 percent of the contemporary world's food comes from plants domesticated by Amerindian, above all, the potato, the tomato and the maize (corn) plant.[1]

Gardening began with the harvesting of wild grains. This agricultural link continued with yams, "tatos" and fruit trees. By 1500 BC, components of gardens, enclosures, trained vines, vegetables in rows and water began showing up in Egypt. Both medicinal and culinary herbs were important elements of these early gardens. As humankind became more civilized, so did their gardens, which began to be more decorative than solely utilitarian. Gardens went from being outside the village walls to being inside, where they were protected from marauders, and with the passage of time, castle walls changed to manor houses.

When the first European settlers arrived, agricultural activity was already going on in this country. The American Indians had set up a system of crop rotation, burning the land to clear it and enriching the soil. The Indians found corn yields could be increased when squash and beans, known as the "Three Sisters," were added to the planting area. The Three Sisters refers to a planting method in which all the plants exist and benefit one another. Animals found it harder to invade the garden because of the closeness of the plantings. The corn stalk acts as the pole for the beans, the beans add nitrogen to the soil and the squash acts as a ground cover to help the soil retain its moisture.[2] Foraging for edible weeds, onions, mustards, fruits, nuts, roots, tubers and mushrooms was also common. Because of their proximity, the Indians and colonists began to trade fruits, vegetables and seeds.

Old Salem Village, showing a communal vegetable garden.

Settlers brought plants, seeds and arrangements of plants with them. Their first priorities were food and shelter, followed closely by medicinal and seasoning plants. The English settlers, with their gardening traditions, planted in rectangular beds edged with herbs. Food wouldn't change drastically along the Atlantic coastline for generations. Corn was considered an annual grass inferior to their staples of wheat, rye, barley and oats. According to Leah Blackman, in *Farming and Gardening Fifty Years Ago*, written between 1860 and 1880, "At that period of time farmers raised clover, grass, Indian corn, wheat, rye (then the great standby for bread), oats, barley, flax and various kinds of vegetables."[3]

Native plants were identified and used for food, medicine and ornamentals.

A Legacy of the Landscape

A communal garden located at Old Salem Village, Winston-Salem, North Carolina.

Since the early seventeenth century, food traditions have influenced the diversity of food plants cultivated and imported to North America, which resulted in an early blending of Native American and European foods that continue to evolve with immigration and cultural changes.[4]

Ornamental gardens were remembrances of home and family in another land. The first homesteads were practical, with "dooryards," an area of the property where daily living activities took place. Blackman describes the dooryard as follows:

Many farm houses had ample front yards about them, but no one presumed on such a thing as having flowering shrubs or plants in the door-yard; such things were assigned to the cultivation of ornamental shrubs plants and medicinal herbs.[5]

The garden was usually located behind the house, with fruit trees located in the dooryard area. Outbuildings were placed to shield the house against the weather.

By the eighteenth century, towns included orchards, which cost many hours of hard work. Trees were planted for shade, decorative purposes and as boundary lines, using seeds and saplings collected from the wild. Trees were also planted to celebrate significant events like births and weddings.

Beans growing at Colonial Williamsburg.

A Legacy of the Landscape

More formal garden style from Colonial Williamsburg at the Governor's Palace.

Blackman noted that "red cedars were the only evergreen trees that then grew in farm house yards, and on them congregated the cedar and other birds that built their nests among the thick foliage."[6] Typically, trees flanked the house, helping to provide shelter. Garden design varied according to taste; however, European tradition was still prominent, as was the use of native species in the landscape. Trial and error, learning what plants would survive and which could be used as substitutes, were commonplace in order to get the desired effect.

Magazines, household manuals and agricultural texts encouraged the concept of well-maintained landscapes in the early nineteenth century. Gardening became part of the social reform movement, which considered it a good and moral activity for women. By the late 1800s, gardening went to the extreme, with the use of bright colors in elaborate beds becoming the preferred style. Gardening became more of a leisure activity. Topiary work, the training and trimming of woody plants used as hedges, screens, arches and arbors became popular. Although the working class had little ornamentation in their gardens, these stylish effects began to creep in their gardens as plants became more affordable.

According to Bernard McMahon, an early Philadelphia nurseryman, in *The American Gardener's Calendar*, written in 1806:

As to the situation of this [kitchen] *garden, with respect to the other districts, if designed principally as a Kitchen and fruit-garden, distinct from the other parts, and that there is room for choice of situation, it should generally be placed detached entirely from the pleasure-ground; also as much out of view of the front of the habitation as possible, at some reasonable distance, either behind it, or towards either side thereof, so as its walls or other fences may not obstruct any desirable prospect either of the pleasure-garden, fields, or the adjacent country.*[7]

The kitchen garden would contain frequently used, easy-to-grow vegetables like amaranth (eaten like spinach), cabbages, pumpkins, squash, artichokes, fennel, beans, peas and lettuce. Tomatoes weren't commonly used in the garden until after 1830. "Tomatoes and egg-plants were not cultivated as they are now."[8]

Root crops, or scarcity roots due to their ability to supply food in times of severe shortages, consisted of potatoes, parsnips, radishes, turnips and carrots. These would be part of a larger garden planted farther from the house due to growing requirements. Root crops also stored well. These would have easy access from the main house because of their almost daily

A combination of plantings showing strawflowers and bird peppers at Old Salem Village, Winston-Salem, North Carolina.

use in cooking. McMahon suggested, when planting carrots and parsnips in this area, "to break all the lumps, that the roots may have full liberty to run down long and straight; for if the earth is not well divided and separated, the roots are apt to grow both short and forked."[9]

Salsify, also known as goat's beard or oyster plant because of its similar taste and texture to oysters, was another popular root. This vegetable, as McMahon describes, "is estimable both for its roots as above, and for the young shoots rising in the spring from the year-old plants, being gathered while green and tender."[10] Pehr Kalm, a Swedish plant explorer working with Carl Linnaeus, visiting America between 1748 and 1751, noted that "potatoes are generally planted. Some people preferred ashes to sand for keeping them in the winter."[11] Corn would be located in the same area. In a diary entry for October 1748, Kalm also noted the following about growing corn:

> *A soil like this in New Jersey, one might be led to think, could produce nothing, because it is dry and poor. Yet the maize, which is planted on it, grows extremely well, and we saw many fields filled with it.*[12]

He also observed at the same time a farming method in which rye was planted between the rows of corn so that, when the corn was harvested, the rye continued to grow.

Herbs were part of the kitchen garden, intermixed with the vegetables. One must remember, in colonial times the herb garden consisted of medicinal, culinary and dye plants. Medicinal herbs were usually located along edges of planting beds. Again, McMahon offers his advice: "part are edged with undershrubby aromatic herbs, as thyme, savory, hyssop, and the like; but unless these are kept low and neat, they appear unsightly."[13] As time progressed and more people lived in town, the herb garden became almost exclusively stocked for culinary purposes with a few simple medicinal herbs. This garden would contain parsley, chamomile, mint, thyme, sage and many of the same herbs we use today.

Around 1820, flowers started to become more prevalent in the garden, with the garden becoming mostly ornamental by 1847. According to Blackman,

> *The flowering plants were daffodils, both white and yellow, snowdrops, bluebells, tulip, and a single light purple hyacinth called sweet Jessie, and sometimes Jacob's ladder, and peonies, pinks of many colors, sweet Williams, mullen pinks, Indian pinks, jump-up-Johnnies, Job's tears,*

Cardoon growing in a Colonial Williamsburg garden.

pheasants eyes, single larkspurs, single hollyhocks, morning glories and bouncing Betties.[14]

Apples were considered an everyday fruit, and all homes had at least one tree. "It will plant and maintain itself,"[15] Alice Morse Earle said of the apple tree in her book, *Old Time Gardens*. The fruit had several uses, including being eaten right off the tree, dried or baked. Blackman noted that "large quantities of apples and peaches were cut and dried for winter use, and dried apple pies and sauce and dried peach pies and sauce were a great institution among all classes."[16] In an October 1748 diary entry, Kalm wrote, "Most of them are winter fruit, and therefore were yet quite sour." They stored well, but there was another use, as Earle described:

The cellar also contained many barrels of cider; for the beauty of the Apple trees, and the use of their fruit as food, were not the only factors which influenced the planting of the many Apple orchards of the new world; they afforded a universal drink—cider.[17]

Sweet and hard cider became the United States' most popular drink by 1820. It was so popular that "many temporizers who tried to exclude cider from the list of intoxicating drinks which converts pledged themselves to abandon."[18]

A Legacy of the Landscape

Blackman noted, "From my earliest recollection I have been accustomed to hearing the cider produced about Newark, New Jersey, extolled for its excellent quality far above that made in any other part of the world." Prior to 1900, there were seven thousand varieties of apple trees available; now there are five main apple varieties.

As mentioned previously, another tree commonly found in the orchard was the peach tree. The timber from peach trees was often used as firewood. Often used as a living fence for boundaries, the trees' fruit was often dried, utilized as livestock fodder or made into brandy and mobby, a juice made from peaches that was sometimes distilled. "The peach was one of our first naturalized weeds, so precocious and abundant, so curiously yet delightfully out of place to European observers."[19] The peach tree was so abundant that even John Bartram, America's pioneering botanist, thought it was a native. Pehr Kalm, in his diary, noted that Bartram "looked upon peaches as an original American fruit, and as growing wild in the greatest part of America."[20] Peachfield Plantation, in Westampton Township, was known for its peach tree *allée* leading up to the house. The double-flowering peach tree was used exclusively as an ornamental hedge.

Cherry, pears, plums and apricots might also be part of the orchard, depending on the owner's circumstances. Cherries were considered culinary luxury trees. They were the third most common fruit tree found in an orchard. Cherry trees were highly prized as ornamental trees, usually lining the edges of the kitchen garden. The pear tree was also considered a fruit tree of the leisure class. A drink, called Perry, was made when the Perry pear was crushed. Pear trees were European and didn't do well in the United States. The climate, along with the disease fire blight, a bacterial infection giving the appearance of scorched leaves, twigs and branches of entire trees that causes sudden wilt, was a problem with the European imports. Fire blight is an American disease and was unknown to the European trees at this time.

Quince was popular before 1800. The fruit from these plants was not tasty by itself, but when used in pies, jellies, preserves and drinks it became quite palatable. Peter Hatch, in *The Fruits and Fruit Tree of Monticello*, wrote, "The quince was no prize but rather a simple and useful addition most common in the farmyards of the middle class."[21] The root stock of the quince was later used in grafting pear trees. Plums were native to the United States but were hard to grow in cultivation. The fruit was used dried. Apricots didn't become common in the garden until about 1800, when they were often used as espaliered landscape specimens.

Small fruits, strawberries, currants, gooseberries and raspberries were often found in a square-over-square planting plan, or berry squares, in the kitchen garden. This plan featured planting beds shaped in squares placed next to one another, with walkways in between. The squares would then be divided in quadrants, with different types of berries located together. Sometimes, in the middle of the square, a fruit tree would be located. Strawberries, being good producers, were cherished wild plants of the meadows and the field. As strawberries became cultivated, they were known as the juiciest and softest of the small fruits. The Lewis and Clark expedition introduced the currant to the berry square. Raspberries were criticized as not tasting as good as the European varieties, where they were considered a wild bramble and not part of the cultivated garden. According to Blackman, "most gardens had a few currant and gooseberry bushes, and some had raspberries and a few strawberries."[22]

Grapes were another fruit that was hard to grow in the U.S. climate, although there were many native grapes that seemed to have no problem. Blackman noted that "cultivated grapes were scarcely known and people depended on the wild grapes of the woods and swamps, and these they considered excellent because they did not know of anything that was better."[23] Most significant grape diseases, black rot and powdery mildew, were native to the United States. By grafting the European rootstock onto the native grape woodstock, disease resistance increased. Grapes were either

An espaliered apple tree at Reynolda Gardens in Winston-Salem, North Carolina.

espaliered or trellised, meaning vines were trained to the lowest rail and eventually encompassed the whole rail, in a vineyard area in the kitchen garden. This area would ideally have a southern exposure, with the ground descending away for drainage. Two basic types of grapes, table and wine, were planted. In Nathan Dunn's garden, his gardener, William H. Carse, was noted in the *Magazine of Horticulture, Botany, and all Useful Discoveries and Improvements in Rural Affairs* for the Pennsylvania Horticultural Society's 1843 Garden Show for growing five varieties of grapes, which included a mixture of wine and table grapes.

As the Industrial Revolution progressed, changes in gardening continued. However, the need for fresh vegetables and fruits did not change. (Remember, grocery stores and convenience stores are all modern conveniences.) Besides the garden, people raised chickens, pigs or cattle. Dovecotes, rabbitries and fish ponds are listed on site plans of large estates, not only as decorative elements, but as edible ones as well. Where—in town or on a farm—and when you lived would also be a consideration in available food. As you can see, vegetable gardens and orchards were very important features to the homes of those living in early times. Plantations, as well as smaller homes, all had some type of garden. The size of the property accounted for what would be grown on the premises. Agriculture was, and still is, a very necessary part of one's survival.

Let's Get Started

Landscape architecture and the nurturing of plants has long been a primary concern and avocation of citizens of Mount Holly. The gardens of the John Woolman house have been a drawing card for visitations to Mount Holly. For many years the gardens of Sarah Leeds and Edward H. Levis drew tourists from "near and far." The garden of Mr. Edward B. Jones still exists with many hundreds of species of trees, plants and flowers and provides an ecological balance within the confines of the town. The wild flower of the Misses Etris at the Samuel Carr house has also been a source of joy for many.[24]

Mount Holly started with an oak tree, kind of. Yes, a group of settlers sailed to Burlington from England on the *Kent* and disembarked. And yes, three of them, John Cripps, his son Nathaniel and Edward Gaskill, took some time to get to Mount Holly, but they made it. The survey for John Cripps's three hundred acres included the following information:

> *It reaches the said creek againe, through which a swamp where grows a store of holley to a white oak by the creek marked as before, within which tract of land is a mountaine to which the province, east, south and west and north sends a beautiful aspect named by the owner thereof Mount Holly.*[25]

This oak, known as the Cripps's Oak according to local tradition, was located at the intersection of Branch Street and Garden Street. However, it is possible that this oak was the wrong oak. The correct oak could have been located farther south; nonetheless, one of the first boundaries in Mount Holly started with an oak tree.

Because of its waterways, Mount Holly began attracting mill and manufacturing industries. The town began growing around the creek once taverns and mills were built. By 1731, the estimated population was approximately 231. Over time, the industries, starting with the gristmills and sawmills, changed to paper mills and thread manufacturing. The name of the town went through changes, as well, starting with Mount Holly, then Northampton, then Bridgetown (because of all the bridges crossing the creek) and finally back to Mount Holly by 1760.

According to Dr. Zachariah Read, as noted in the Cripps survey, the town was originally named for "the Mount" covered with holly: "The Mount in the distance covered with trees and the valley near the creek thickly studded with the beautiful Holly is without doubt the source whence the place was named."[26] There is some speculation that the Mount was confused with another hill, Top E Toy, because of its proximity to the Cripps property. According to Henry Shinn, in his book *The History of Mount Holly*, the Mount is 185 feet above sea level.

THE ROSSELLS

I will begin Mount Holly's gardening history with a tavern. Zachariah Rossell owned the Black Horse Tavern, built before the Revolution. The tavern was a stagecoach stop on the road to Philadelphia. Rossell was a highly regarded citizen, with his name appearing among those who started the library and the schoolhouse on Brainerd Street. He also served in the Revolutionary War. Because of his service and outspokenness against the British, his home and buildings were plundered, and he was taken prisoner. Rossell owned the tavern for fifty years, until he retired to his home on High Street. The following is a brief description of Zachariah:

> *Next is the homestead of Zachariah Rossell, here the old gentleman retires, after the active duties of life were over, and passed his days in quiet, he was a man who took an active part in the sturing* [sic] *events of the day, possessed of a sound mind.*[27]

He died in 1815.

His son, William, trained to be a harness maker; however, he became the surrogate of Monmouth County. Eventually, he was appointed judge of the United States for the District of New Jersey and associate judge of the Supreme Court of New Jersey, serving twenty-two years in all. He was said to have been the only judge ever chosen who wasn't a licensed lawyer. He was appointed by President John Quincy Adams. He had seven children,

A Legacy of the Landscape

New Jersey–native azaleas and rhododendrons in a backyard.

and he owned a large portion of Mount Holly. When he died in 1840, his land was divided into parcels for his children and grandchildren.

> *The next lot and upon which the Mount Holly and Burlington Railroad is built, was the property of Zachariah Rossell, who gave it with other property to his son William Rossell, who gave it to his daughter Mrs. Catherine Allen.*[28]

Throughout this book, there will be many references to William Rossell as being the former owner of land purchased by others.

In the research material used to write this book, the only reference I could find in regards to the Rossell property is about grapes. The following is one of two references:

> *The mountain slope of the south is a part of the Rossell Estate, on a part of which Mr. Wm. Rossell has an extensive grapery, and for some years made considerable wine, this wine was said to be excellent, and those who were fortunate as to get a taste always praised it as a most delicious beverage, and some were extravagant enough to describe it to be equal to any imported from abroad.*[29]

A New Jersey–native rhododendron in flower.

A Legacy of the Landscape

The other reference talks about the man who attended to the grapery, Josiah O. Priest.

I wanted to take the time to introduce the Rossell family, as the name appears quite often in other chapters of the book. I also felt that starting off with a little history of the town wouldn't hurt either. Mount Holly has an exciting historical past covering most aspects of American history in one way or another. Quite a few colorful characters have lived here. The many gardens of Mount Holly were some of the most beautiful around, ranging across different time spans. Unfortunately, this book only holds a few, but they are among the most notable that could be found.

John Woolman's Garden

He declared that there he found health both physical and spiritual. Once he said: "If the things of the Spirit were more attended to, more people would be engaged in the sweet employment of husbandry, where labor is agreeable and healthful."[30]

John Woolman, one of Mount Holly's foremost citizens, was best known as a humanitarian and abolitionist. Woolman lived in Mount Holly starting about 1741. He was born in 1720 on his father's farm, located along the Rancocas Creek six miles outside of town, close to Rancocas Village. The family farm, established in 1678, was "where his father made a great feature of his orchard."[31]

Woolman's mother, Elizabeth Burr, was the eldest daughter of prominent plantation owner, Henry Burr, and his wife, Elizabeth. The family owned a 300-acre property known as Peachfields, purchased in 1695 from the widow of the former owner, John Skene. George Decou notes that "John Skene purchased the plantation, then supposed to contain 250 acres, from Edward Byllynge, one of the original purchasers of West Jersey 'by lease and release' on 'the 14th and 15th of the Fourth month, 1682.'"[32] What I find most interesting about these old surveys is their use of trees and other plants as markers; in this case, "from Samuel Jennings corner stake south east fifty seven chains to a white oak marked for corner."[33]

In 1714, Burr purchased an additional two hundred acres. The family lived in a nearby house on the property until two sections, the eastern and central, of their stone mansion, an unusual feature for this time, were built in 1725. The western section was added in 1732 by Burr's son, John, the former surveyor general of West Jersey (1716).

Peachfield Plantation's square-over-square herb garden.

A fire gutted the interior of the house in 1929, leaving only the fireplaces and lower portions of the walls. The remains stood abandoned for a number of years, until the property was purchased in 1931 by the Harkers, who hired R. Borgnard Okie, an architect who was well known for Colonial Revival country houses and restoration work. The building and grounds are now the headquarters for the Colonial Dames in the State of New Jersey. The building stands on a knoll surrounded by fields and a golf course. When I was given a tour, my guide talked about a peach tree *allée* running parallel to the golf course. The front grounds are almost a miniature arboretum, with labels on the tree specimens. In late spring, the beds are a multitude of color because of the massive amounts of irises and peonies. At the back of the grounds is a small colonial-style square-over-square herb garden.

Currently, plans are under way to build a wing onto the house to represent the two-car garage that was once part of the original Okie plans. The gardens are transitioning, as happens, with a tea garden replacing the herb garden and more demonstration gardens featuring crops, like in the Old Salem Village in Winston-Salem, North Carolina. Another feature, a boxwood-lined memorial, illustrates how graves would have been placed on a plantation during its prime. I should note that the memorial at Peachfield

A Legacy of the Landscape

An herb garden at Peachfield Plantation in Westampton, New Jersey.

is not a grave, but a Masonic memorial. I like to use it as an example to illustrate the following characteristic: "In the middle of the eighteenth century, colonial gardeners occasionally designed areas of their grounds in honor of a special friend or relative, often one who had recently died."[34] The building and grounds are open to visitors by appointment.

Like many men of his time, Woolman apprenticed with a local storeowner to learn shopkeeping. Eventually, in 1747, he purchased a house with a small building for his shop, but he gave up shopkeeping after he realized that making money interfered too much with his spirituality. Instead, he learned the tailoring trade. He sold the property to his mother, Elizabeth. He supplemented his income with surveying, writing legal documents and tending his orchard. While in his twenties, he became a local minister for the Society of Friends; his traveling ministry began by age twenty-six. In 1749, he married and had two daughters, only one of whom survived to adulthood. By 1756, Woolman's main occupations were tailoring and taking care of his orchard while traveling for his ministry.

John Woolman's opposition to slavery led to his appointment as head of a committee that spoke to all Friends who held slaves in order to get them to stop in 1758. He strove to separate himself from slavery and the slave trade

John Woolman's garden, from a postcard owned by the author.

by not using sugar, molasses or other products made by slaves. He refused to wear dyed clothing, another byproduct of slave labor, and he refused to be a guest in houses in which slaves were held.

Woolman purchased two hundred acres along the Rancocas, where he built a modest home before he married in 1748. The exact location is not known, although it is mentioned in several books that the house was located on top of a hill. He planted a garden and an orchard of apple trees. "In the nursery, he said, I employed some of my time in hoeing, grafting trimming, and inoculating."[35] He enjoyed his time in the orchard immensely. In 1771, he built a home for his daughter adjacent to the one in which he lived. These are now part of "the John Woolman Memorial."

A description of the garden as it looked in 1932 is included in the book, *Old Gardens In and About Philadelphia* (1936):

> *The two houses are in the old garden which runs back nine hundred feet from the road. There is a quaint old well, an arbor to which the roses cling lovingly. The walled terrace and the apple trees in the lower end of the garden are very beautiful at all seasons, but especially in apple-blossom time. Old-fashioned flowers are everywhere. One of the charms of the whole is the seeming lack of order that helps to emphasize the random beauty of the whole.*[36]

John Woolman's garden from *Old Gardens In and About Philadelphia. Courtesy of the Rancocas Historical Society.*

Behind the meetinghouse, showing the buttonwood trees planted at the same time as the building.

A Legacy of the Landscape

There is another reference to the garden in George DeCou's book: "The Association conducts a tea room in the old building and whether Friend or non-Friend, a cup of tea by the old well in the beautiful garden."[37]

John Woolman died in 1772 of smallpox while on a missionary trip to England. He is buried in York, England. Behind the Friend's meetinghouse, one can see his memorial stone, along with his wife's, who is buried there, right inside the fence. Farther up Branch Street, the John Woolman Memorial still stands as a monument to this peace-loving man. The quaint well, along with boxwood-lined beds and apple trees, grace the yard at the memorial even now. His journal of religious travels and inner experiences has been in print since 1774.

> *Evidently daily views of the paths and the flowers that tell of the Quaker garden of days before the Revolution was effective in inspiring her* [referring to Miss Sarah Leeds, a neighbor of the Memorial site] *to continue the tradition of the favored country by the Rancocas.*[38]

Both buildings and gardens still exist and are open to visitors by appointment. The Woolman garden is undergoing renovation by the Burlington County Master Gardeners.

Timbuctoo

I wanted to touch briefly on a community located about a mile outside of Mount Holly called Timbuctoo, or "Buckto." When I first thought about writing something about this community and its gardens, it was looked upon as a little strange, as this book is mostly about large and formal gardens. As an African American community, started sometime between 1820 and 1825, it was a haven for freedmen, as well as fugitive slaves. Any gardens located there would have been mainly for survival—gardens of subsistence. The town was located in a wooded area and was a stop on the underground railroad. Mount Holly had two other stops, the Ashurst Mansion and a small wooded area not far from the mansion, both of which will be discussed further later on.

Many of the men of the community had jobs in Mount Holly, but they were of the manual type that came with low pay. In order to survive, a garden could provide food and a possible source of income when the overstock was sold or bartered. Good soil, rich in organic matter, loose in texture and well drained, along with the right sun exposure, preferably on a south-facing slope, were and still are the necessary ingredients for a bountiful garden. The location, where the garden could be protected, was another part of the recipe. Rudy Favretti observed the following:

> It is interesting to note here that the basic principles for the establishment and laying out of the common garden—soil, exposure, relationship to the dwelling house—also applied to the laying out of gardens on estates, or places grander than the common garden. The concept seems to apply throughout all types of garden styles and design.[39]

These spaces were planted intensively and randomly to maximize the space.

Even though this community was located in a Northern state, the food would be cooked in a more flavorful style. Boiling and baking vegetables and meats were the usual style of cooking, with little to no adventure taken outside these confines, thereby maintaining the cook's piousness. People who cooked in a more Southern tradition were not afraid to experiment, to use an assortment of herbs, spices and plants.

Items commonly found in these gardens were potatoes, sweet potatoes, pumpkins, winter squash and cabbages, all of which stored well for winter. Greens, summer squash, eggplants and melons were eaten fresh, with beans and peas eaten either fresh or dried. Okra, used in soups as a thickener, was noted by Peter Kalm in his travels in the area: "Fruit, which is a long pod, is cut while it is green and boiled in soups, which thereby become as thick as porridge. This dish is reckoned a dainty by some people."[40] Tomatoes were still an oddity, but again, because of the willingness to experiment, they made their way into the pots of the Southern food traditionalists.

Inedible decorative gourds were also grown for use as bowls, skimmers, dippers and bottles. Small orchards with apples and peaches would be located nearby, again because of their storage and preservation capabilities. Grains, rye, barley, corn, sunflowers and hops were grown for the use of the community, but they could also be sold. The gathering of nature's bounty from the woods—hickory nuts, berries, various herbs and grasses, goosefoot, pokeweed, smartweed—was another way to increase the foodstuffs. Most medicinals were herbs grown in the garden or gathered.

All that remains of this community is its small cemetery, which I recently visited for a Memorial Day service honoring the Civil War soldiers buried there. It was the first time I had been back there, and I was most impressed with the area. No buildings remain, just the cemetery. Standing there during the service under a hickory tree, with a squirrel throwing nuts at me, I decided to write this small piece about what might have been in their gardens, even though they weren't formal or ornate.

America's First Millionaire

If I thought I was going to die tomorrow, I should plant a tree, nevertheless, today.[41]

This chapter is about Stephen Girard, America's first millionaire. The time he spent in Mount Holly was short, but I will try to describe what his garden here was like. Please keep in mind that, though Girard was born in Bordeaux, France, in 1750, he did not personify the French "dandy." He maintained a working-class ethic throughout his life. His garden would not have been typical of the French garden style. There would be no topiaries, no parterres. He was a very hardworking man who became very active in his adopted country even before he became an official citizen. Girard was the oldest of nine children born to a seafaring family. His mother died when he was twelve. With no formal schooling and no vision in his right eye, Girard continued the family tradition by going to sea at age thirteen. By age twenty-three, he was a captain licensed by the French merchant marine.

In the midst of the Revolutionary War, Girard came to Philadelphia because of the British blockade of New York Harbor. He sailed up the Delaware River into the Philadelphia Harbor. This is where he decided to make his permanent home. This was also when he met Isaac Hazlehurst, a Mount Holly resident who eventually partnered with Girard, along with a third person, in the shipping industry while Girard captained the ships. As Girard became more comfortable with his entrepreneurial abilities, the partnership was gradually phased out.

Girard opened a shop in Philadelphia in 1777. This is also when he married. Because of his concerns about the British occupation of Philadelphia, coupled with the fact that he was a French citizen who helped supply the American forces with food and whatever else he could get through

The Girard house today.

the blockades, Girard and his wife, Mary, decided to leave Philadelphia and move to Mount Holly. He set up shop at 211 Mill Street, noted as being a fine example of a working man's house from 1733, after he acquired the five-acre property from Hazlehurst. From his basement shop, he continued his support of Washington's troops, whose function was to harass the British in the South Jersey area. Mount Holly's local residents also benefitted from the shop, where the shelves were filled with whatever Girard could get through the blockades.

By mid-1778, the British occupied Mount Holly. This is the same time Girard "disappeared" from town. His abrupt departure made for some interesting stories. The first is related to his wife, who was very much an extrovert, and a pretty one as well. Girard walked into his shop to witness his wife receiving a kiss from either a Continental or a British colonel (there's a "kiss" story for both sides). The second is related to his snapping and barking dog. On one occasion, the dog attached himself to a man's pant leg. The man kicked the dog across the floor, threatening death if the dog did it again. Sure enough, the dog again attached himself to the man's pant leg, resulting in the canine's premature death. It was said that Girard left because he could not "live among such ungrateful people."[42] The last and most likely reason was the fact that the British had left Philadelphia. Girard was free to return to the city and his business activities. Girard became an American citizen in 1778. Interestingly, he also added more acreage to his Mount Holly property in 1779.

For the next six years, Girard and his wife continued their business in Philadelphia, with occasional visits to Mount Holly. In 1785, Mary began showing signs of mental illness, exhibiting periods of emotional outbursts often accompanied by violent rages. Girard took her for diagnosis, but instead of having her committed right away, he sent her to Mount Holly. He "hoped the restful setting on the five-acre tract, offering open spaces, a change of scenery and the respite from the hustle and bustle of a congested city, would make her feel better."[43]

Girard's Mount Holly property was to be a restful sanctuary for his wife. Mount Holly was considered by some Philadelphians to be a rustic location where one could escape the summer heat of the city. With Girard's property backing up to Isaac Hazlehurst's and Buttonwood Run, it is more than likely that Girard kept the back of the property in a natural style. This would be the same style in which Hazlehurst kept his, a natural oasis. Hazlehurst also helped with the care of Girard's wife at times during her visits to Mount Holly. The gardens "were meant to walk in, and most of them had a road system that meandered the boundary of the park from which one could get glimpses of the landscape within the garden, as well as, without."[44]

Other common elements of a wealthy merchant's garden might have been a central walkway ending in a focal point, a summerhouse or an arbor, for example. Beds for flowers, lining either side of the walkway, in addition to trees, either fruit or shade, if space permitted, would be another feature. Of course, a fence would be included, as well. In Girard's case, most probably a picket or board type. Girard kept the Mount Holly property until 1790, the same year he had Mary institutionalized. He had tried to take care of her as best he could, but once she started wandering away, he felt he had no choice. Mary was admitted to Pennsylvania Hospital, where she was given every luxury available. She died in September 1815.

Behind the Girard house today.

Although Girard left Mount Holly, he did maintain business relationships with many of the local merchants. It is noted in one of his datebooks that he purchased fruit trees from the area. His businesses also allowed him the opportunity to import seeds and plants from overseas, also noted in his datebooks. His interest in working the soil led him to purchase a farm in Philadelphia, as stated previously. His farm consisted of seventy-five acres. Henry Seckel, who introduced and grew the Seckel pear, was a previous owner. Girard ran the farm, as he did all his businesses, for a profit.

In 1830, the Horticultural Society of Pennsylvania recognized the farm for being the best. The report said that twenty acres of the farm were divided into an orchard and a vegetable farm, and this acreage was enclosed by a board fence. The orchard included Seckel pears and other pear varieties imported from France, and the collection was "second to none in this country." The society reported that Girard was one of the first to use turpentine and bandages to heal tree wounds. The garden comprised an acre and a half of fine vegetables, "including America's first artichokes and a variety of imported grape vines."[45] When he died in 1831, his farm amounted to 583 acres.

A Legacy of the Landscape

Dogwoods, another New Jersey native, in bloom across several backyards.

Dogwood in bloom in Atlanta, Georgia.

Captain William Rogers purchased the house in 1812 in Mount Holly, and it remained in the family for several generations. The house had a porch added and an addition, which nearly doubled its size to what we see today. The house is still standing and is privately owned.

Clover Hill /
Ashurst Mansion

Of all the faculties of the human mind that of Memory is the first which suffers decay from age.
—*Thomas Jefferson to Benjamin Henry Latrobe, Monticello, July 12, 1812*

The house is all that remains of this estate, also known as Clover Hill. The estate occupied a large amount of the land just outside of central Mount Holly. There are many local legends attached to this property. I will try to discuss several in this space.

Isaac Hazelhurst was born in England in 1742. He trained as a merchant and, in 1768, immigrated to Philadelphia, where, along with his thirteen-year-old brother Robert, he became quite successful. He married in 1769 and, together with his wife Juliana, had seven children. About 1774, Hazelhurst came to Mount Holly to find a place far enough away from the Revolutionary War to be safe. He purchased considerable amounts of property, including the Mount (which became the Mount Farm), another farm and a landing lot on the Rancocas, where he had his household supplies shipped, plus additional pieces located throughout the town. Although he was English, Hazelhurst remained loyal to his adopted country, contrary to several things written about him being a Loyalist. During his tenure in Mount Holly, his home was occupied by Lord Cornwallis, Sir Henry Clinton and their staffs on more than one occasion. We do know that there was an orchard on the property by the following excerpt from Henry Shinn's book: "Upon the approach of the British the family jewelry, silver, and other valuables were buried, some in the orchard, some in the garden, and in other places."[46] In 1777, Hazlehurst's friend, Stephan Girard, bought his Mill Street property, also to escape the Revolutionary War in Philadelphia.

The Hazelhurst summerhouse. *Courtesy of the Mount Holly Historical Society.*

A Legacy of the Landscape

The property was kept in the naturalistic style popular at this time. One significant feature was a summerhouse, which, according to legend, was a spot where Washington and Lafayette held councils of war. The summerhouse was originally located on Hazlehurst's Philadelphia property. It was a wooden structure with a Chinese fretwork design and benches inside. It was dismantled and shipped to Mount Holly about 1800 by one of Hazlehurst's granddaughters. According to the Historic American Building Survey done on the structure in 1938, the summerhouse was really built in about 1854. In a news article, the summerhouse is mentioned as follows: "The famous summerhouse, now standing in the centre of the wooded grove back of the mansion, is their pride and care."[47] It remained in Mount Holly for a century and a half before it was shipped to Pennsylvania and finally to New York in the 1940s.

Isaac Hazlehurst had three business centers, in Philadelphia, New Orleans and Charleston, the latter of which his brother ran. Hazlehurst was a merchant with interests in shipping. Stephen Girard had partnered with him in a few ventures before starting his own business. Because of the economic conditions in 1808, after the passing of the 1807 Embargo Act, as well as the War of 1812, Hazlehurst retired to Clover Hill. After the War of 1812, his son, Samuel, recovered the family fortune. He retained the Philadelphia business, while his brother kept the Charleston one. His brother moved back to the area in 1824 and settled in Burlington.

Hazlehurst's eldest and only daughter, Mary Elizabeth, married Benjamin Henry Boneval Latrobe, America's first fully trained architect, in 1800. Latrobe came to the United States in 1796, arriving first in Virginia. He was the son of a Moravian minister in Leeds, Yorkshire, England. He initially studied engineering, but became interested in architecture following a trip to Germany. His architectural style of choice, Greek Revival, was becoming quite popular in the United States at this same time. He worked on several projects in the Norfolk and Richmond area, including the state penitentiary in Richmond, where he advocated for penal reform. After visiting Philadelphia in 1798, Latrobe decided to move his practice to Philadelphia, where he built up his reputation. He received the commission to design the Bank of Pennsylvania, which was torn down in 1870, and the Fairmount Water Works, among other buildings.

In 1803, Latrobe was hired as surveyor of public buildings of the United States by Thomas Jefferson. He oversaw the construction of the capitol building, as well as several others in the country's capital. From 1803 to 1808, he had an assistant, Robert Mills, working with him; another person connected to Mount Holly. Mills was the designer of the Burlington County

Historic Prison, a commission he received through his association with Latrobe. Many of Latrobe's ideas of penal reform were instituted with Mill's design. Latrobe resigned as surveyor in 1817. He and Mary had five children through their marriage. Latrobe died of yellow fever while working in New Orleans on a water plant in 1820. I am sure that Latrobe visited Mount Holly on occasion, but there is one documented visit recorded by Dr. Read: "He [Isaac Hazelhurst] became possessed of much land…By a map made in 1801 by Benjamin Henry Latrobe, Esq."[48] In the condition assessment for the library, this map is remarked upon in the following way:

> *It is interesting to ask what Benjamin Latrobe was doing surveying a rural estate in Mount Holly with no associated architectural commission. He may have been doing a favor for his father-in-law.*[49]

One of the many properties Isaac Hazelhurst owned was the Mount, or Mount Farm as it was called. In 1829, he was paid $1,000 for the timber on the Mount. This seemed to cause a bit of controversy, according to Henry Shinn, "and the ancient holly trees were destroyed."[50] Dr. Read was a bit gentler when he wrote:

> *It was covered by a thick growth of wood fifty years, since and was cut off about thirty years ago by Josiah Zelley, a merchant of Mount Holly, who gave Mr. Hazelhurst $1000 for the wood, since which time it is fast growing up again.*[51]

The Hazelhurst estate sold the Mount property to Reverend Isaac Brown in 1837, three years after Hazelhurst died. The Mount will be discussed in further detail in the next chapter.

After Hazelhurst's death, the property went to his first son, Samuel, who died in 1849. His second son, Robert, had died in 1804. The estate remained in the family through his daughter, Mary, who married Lewis Richard Ashurst. It was at this point that the estate, after the old house was torn down, became known as Ashurst Mansion. The bricks for the construction were imported from England, with a coat of arms over the portico. The most interesting feature, according to local tradition, and noted in Mary Smith's book, are the "passages in the cellar [that] lead into at least two tunnels now closed that were used by escaping slaves before the Civil War, so oral history reports."[52] Supposedly, the second tunnel led out to the gazebo, which, as stated before, was set apart from the house in a wooded area. Smith's book also suggests that the house was a stop on the underground railroad:

The Hazelhurst Mansion. *Courtesy of the Mount Holly Historical Society from the Cowgill Scrapbook.*

It would appear there could be a strong reason to believe that the Ashurst Mansion and the property at 427 Garden Street were both stops on the Underground Railroad. The area was a strong Quaker community; the area was on the underground route, both properties were close to each other, the Mansion was surrounded by woods, which came into proximity to the Garden Street property. Timbuctoo, a black settlement, was a short distance away from the two locations and not heavily populated.[53]

The mansion is in the Gothic Revival style with thirty-four rooms. The following buildings were located on the property: a brick milk house, a bathhouse, a schoolhouse, a wood house and workshop and, of course, the greenhouse. "The beautiful wooded area coming from the rear of the mansion on East Garden Street out to Clover Street was a section of paths, small pools, wonderful ornamental trees, and wild flowers." In 1905, there was a note in the *New Jersey Mirror* about the property's buildings being spruced up while the owner was in London. Near the Union Street intersection, the remnants of a gatehouse were still standing in 1955. For a description of the gatehouse, I have chosen this excerpt from the September 15, 1955 *Mount*

Roses in one of the backyards showcased during the Hidden Gardens Tour of Mount Holly. *Courtesy of Larry Tigar.*

Holly Herald: "Old residents may remember the gatekeeper's lodge, with its quaint diamond-shaped window, that stood at the entrance of the driveway into the estate."[54]

Richard, Ashurst's son, lived in Philadelphia with his son, but he summered in Mount Holly. Upon the death of his father, the mansion was placed with a caretaker. It was sold in 1948 to a developer, who built Clover Hill Apartments on part of the estate's land. The house is still standing and is used as offices. There is still a small remembrance of Isaac Hazelhurst and his property: two streets, Garden, named for his large and unusual garden, and Clover, named for his estate, Clover Hill, are still frequently traveled.

Langleland

Burlington County Lyceum of Natural Sciences and History/Mount Holly Library

They walked over the crackling leaves in the garden, between the lines of Box, breathing its fragrance of eternity; for this is one of the odors which carry us out of time into the abysses of the unbeginning past; if we ever lived on another ball of stone than this, it must be that there was Box growing on it. [55]

G lossy spokes of tourmaline green. Tiny jewel-like leaves. The *Buxus sempervirens* is 175 years old, halfway through its lifespan, all seventeen hundred feet of it. It is overgrown yet magnificent, eight feet tall in places, with the usual bitter fragrance. Only one other aged boxwood maze is located in New Jersey, with the number of these antiques getting smaller as time passes. An 1893 picture of the mansion shows the front hedgerow. The Burlington County Lyceum of Natural Science, or the Mount Holly Library as it is better known, started its life as a family home with not much being known about the original owner. This made for a lot of "whys." Putting all the "whys" together with the known bits and pieces, we can get a general idea of what this plantation owner's life was like in the 1830s.

James Langstaff was born into a prominent Mount Holly family. In 1743, a schoolhouse was to be built on "this acre [lying] at N.E. end of Caleb Shreve's Mount."[56] The Langstaff family are listed as participants in this undertaking. The original family home was also on High Street; however, it was closer to the center of town, as noted in Dr. Read's book:

> *Below was a very large brick house, larger by far than any in the place, it stood upon the corner of School Alley* [now Brainerd Street] *and High Street. It was built by John Ridgway, it was long and had a great many windows in it from which circumstance, it was called Ridgway's Althorn, he*

The Mount Holly Library in 1911. *Courtesy of the Mount Holly Library and the Mount Holly Historical Society.*

sold it to one, Hunlock, an Englishman who lived there with his family but he proved to be a British Spy, and had to absquatulate in the night, his property was confiscated, 1779, and sold to George Langstaff, who afterwards lived there, an eminent buttonwood and willow stood in front on School Alley, but James Langstaff inherited it from his father George Langstaff.[57]

His father is listed in early papers as a "planter."

Our particular James Langstaff was born June 16, 1809. By the age of ten, he was an orphan, about the same time as a local typhoid epidemic. His guardian, Joseph Budd, had to go to court for him to save "a certain tract of land and plantation"[58] that was in foreclosure. Family property was also located in Chamber's Corners, not far from Mount Holly, where the lumber to build his home came from. There was a reference to a farm located on Burlington Road, now Route 541. Henry Shinn, referencing another holding owned by Langstaff, wrote:

When navigation on the Rancocas was at its height all supplies for the town were transported by water, requiring numerous landings along the creek. Joseph Willett's and James Langstaff's landings were further east.[59]

A Legacy of the Landscape

Mount Holly Library. *Courtesy of Larry Tigar.*

Langstaff showed up again in the *Mirror* when he married Harriet Haines on April 20, 1830. According to Dr. Read, "Mr. James Langstaff purchased of William Rossell and he erected his spacious house and laid out his extensive garden."[60] He purchased six acres and built his bride a roomy Georgian-style mansion, with an extensive boxwood garden he called "Langleland," Welsh for "a foot of high ground." He was again listed in papers as an "undesignated" county freeholder when it came time to inventory Nathan Dunn's estate upon his death. Dunn resided across the street from the Langstaffs and their four children, George, Annie, Susan and Samuel.

Langstaff preferred the formal Georgian plantings reminiscent of the manor houses in England, Wales and Virginia. His massive boxwood garden, a hedgerow in the front, a maze on the side and an *allée* in the back were all parts of his formal garden. Mazes were part of the pleasure garden but were sometimes also part of the privy garden, meaning they were for the family's use only, which is a possibility here due to the maze's location. The best view of the maze was from the second floor; the library's maze is directly below the master bedroom windows.

Mazes have been around for thousands of years. The earliest recorded one is from an Egyptian temple/palace circa 1795 BC. Mazes became popular ornamental garden features in Italy, then France and finally England. When the British started settling America, they brought with them the landscaping practices with which they were comfortable to create that bit of home in the wilderness. At this time, William, more than Mary, had a liking for boxwood clipped into all shapes and sizes. Labyrinths seemed to fade in and out of use as garden features throughout the next four hundred years. Bernard McMahon observed:

> *Sometimes small labyrinths are formed with box-edgings, and borders for plants, with handsome narrow walks between, in imitations of the larger ones; which have a very pleasing and amusing effect in small gardens.*[61]

Such is the case in the Langstaff garden. A formal Georgian garden (1700–1830) consisted of several elements. "The firm lines of the beautifully clipped box hedges which edge all the paths introduce discipline to the unconstrained shapes."[62] This was a description of the box at Mottisfont Abbey in England. For a local account, McMahon offered, "In imitation of nature…of varied forms and dimensions should be used, and winding walks, all bounded with plantations of trees, shrubs and flowers in various clumps, must be included."[63] Other suggestions included planting clumps of trees and shrubs along the boundaries with annual and perennial flowers mixed in, almost like thickets. Trees with interesting shapes should be intermixed in the open lawn. Some kind of hedge work, whether it be geometric flower beds or parterres, would be part of this garden style. A natural-looking water feature might be a component, as well. Shrubbery would be grouped under trees to create the "understory" effect for a more natural look.

A photo from 1911 shows the front boxwood as knee high, with five arborvitae, or junipers, located in the hedgerow. These are gone now and have been replaced with azaleas mixed in with the boxwood. The hedgerow along the front has encroached on the brick walks leading up to the building. The once-open front entryway of the building has been enclosed. One does notice large stone posts at the curb line, which could indicate where the entrance to the property was, possibly in the form of a semicircular drive.

Another feature in the library garden is the *allée*, a feature of a French formal garden that included a promenade and an extension of the view ending in a terminal feature like a summerhouse. Specimen trees could be included as a possible ending feature for the *allée*. "An overgrown, boxwood-lined path which extends directly on axis with the center hall of the historic building now points to the east door of the assembly room."[64] The *allée* lines up directly with what was once an entryway with a lovely set of hand-painted

The Mount Holly Library today. *Courtesy of Larry Tigar.*

glass side windows. (See photo no. 5 in the center section, showing what it might have looked like through the door before the community room was attached.) Where the community room now stands, there was once a trellis and arbor; both were torn down to make room for the addition in 1967. It has been suggested that

> *the length alone of the boxwood path asks us to consider whether there were perhaps additional formal parterres or a feature (such as a small structure) which terminated the path on the east. The placement of painted glass within the house, particularly the east sidelights of the southeast parlor, further reinforces the notion of an enhanced landscape on the east side of the building* [65]

Boxwood, holly and yew were the plants of choice for these formal gardens, being British natives that were bushy enough to make extensive garden architecture. All are evergreen, immensely long-lived, take clipping well (although boxwood is the least vigorous of the three) and form a dense texture, providing a perfect backdrop for other plants. Boxwood, Langstaff's plant of choice, is most likely a native of North Africa, although there is contention about how it got to England. It was either brought by the Romans or is a native plant to the southern part of England—no one can be sure. Boxwood was brought to the United States by settlers as cuttings to remind them of the elegance of home until a new elegance could be grown in their new country. It is considered a great ornamental plant, taking to topiary work easily. The hard wood is close-grained, having been used for small things like combs and inlays.

The gardens on the property would have been quite extensive. I have already noted the former trellis, with arbor, where the community room is located. In the east garden, a well and grape arbors were said to be located: "A well, readily accessible to the kitchen and located on the southern building exposure, would be most desirable."[66] At least two specimen trees, a copper beech tree and a weeping willow, an indication of where a water feature may have been, still stand on the property. The remaining shrubberies, which seem to be original to the property, are some lilacs and two bottlebrush buckeyes, one in the front of the building, the other in the back. There was a nice stand of dwarf cardamom and daffodils growing in the planting beds on the side of the building where the maze is located. A few still remain. In early spring, one can still witness an ocean of tiny purple crocus covering the east lawn.

The home stayed in the Langstaff family until 1930, when it was purchased by a doctor, who used the building for his home and office. In 1957, the mansion became the first permanent home for the Mount Holly Library. Before that, the library moved around town to various locations. The building and grounds have gone through some changes to make them more adaptable for use as a public building, but much of its charm and character can still be seen. The library staff is willing to take visitors on a tour of this unique structure. It is also a stop on the Haunted Holly tour, as the house is haunted by the ghost of a little girl who died falling from the third-floor open staircase.

Because of all the years without care, the boxwood is showing signs of age and stress. Boxwood can live to be four hundred years old. The library's are mere teenagers, but the older the shrubs become, the harder it becomes for them to regenerate. How does a plant show signs of age? In the library's case, since the boxwood have gotten so tall without clipping, the leaves are all on the outside, meaning that if one looks down inside one of the bushes, she will only see branches and sticks with no leaves. In order to fix that, the shrubs need to be thinned so light and air can get through. The clipping has to be done gradually, taking about six inches off each season. It is a very slow and tedious process. I know. I've been working on it, for the most part alone, for the last couple of years. In the case of the maze, the box shrubs

A Legacy of the Landscape

The entrance to the maze. *Courtesy of Nina Gee.*

have gotten so large that they have encroached on the paths, making it hard to discern the correct passageway, and on one another, causing dieback in some cases.

In a letter written to the American Boxwood Society, dated 1974, there seems to be a concern with insect infestation. The current boxwood have at least one of everything described on the information sheets, but as the bushes get clipped and the inner growth comes back with its green luster, there seems to be less insect damage. There are a lot of unwanted weeds and trees growing amongst the box that affect the air and light flow. The clipped bushes have started to make it more difficult for the weeds to grow as they fill in, but this all takes time. It is rewarding to see how nicely they are taking to what care is given to them now.

The library is another one of the wonderfully rare buildings that make up Mount Holly. Little information is known about the Langstaff property, but I have explained what I can. There is a survey showing the property outline when it was purchased from William Rossell, but this is all that can be found, besides the references in the Read and Shinn books. We can only speculate as to the "whys." Hopefully, some day, we'll be able to find some answers to the many questions. Until then, we can enjoy the gardens and buildings for what they are. Maybe one day the garden will once again reflect the formal Georgian style it started with.

The China-
Mount Holly Connection

To build, to plant, whatever you intend,
To rear the column, or to arch to bend,
To swell the terrase, or to sink the Grot;
in all, let Nature never be forgot.

But treat the goddess like a modest fair,
Nor over-dress, nor leave her wholly bare;
Let not each beauty ev'ry where be spy'd
Where half the skill is decently to hide:
He gains all points, who pleasingly confounds,
Surprizes, varies, and conceals the Bounds.

Consult the genius of the place in all;
That tells the Waters or to rise, or fall,
Or helps th' ambitious Hill the heav'n to scale,
Or scoops in circling Theatres the Vale,
Calls in the country, catches opening glades,
Joins willing woods, and varies shades with shades,
Now breaks, or now directs, th' intending Lines,
Paints as you plant, and as you work, designs.

—Alexander Pope[67]

After William Rossell passed away, his property was divided by his son, Zachariah. Zachariah Rossell kept a tavern, the Black Horse, one of two stagecoach stops in town. Our next gardener, Nathan Dunn, purchased two of these lots, which amounted to a little over twenty-three acres. This is where Nathan Dunn decided to build his escape from the Philadelphia summers, called "The Cottage," located on the edge of Mount Holly.

Let me first introduce you to this interesting man. Nathan Dunn was born September 29, 1782, in Salem County, New Jersey, to a Quaker farming family. His father died shortly after his birth. His mother remarried in 1788. He had two brothers, William and Josiah, and a sister, Deborah, from his mother's first marriage and three sisters, Phebe, Palmyra and Rhoda, from his mother's second marriage.

Dunn's Chinese Cottage in 1860. *Courtesy of the Mount Holly Library.*

A Legacy of the Landscape

A stipulation of Dunn's father's will was that all the boys must learn a trade. After two of the three reached the age of twenty-one, the two-hundred-acre family plantation would be sold, with the proceeds split among the children. In 1802, Dunn moved to Philadelphia, where he apprenticed to a merchant. He also became a member of the Philadelphia Monthly Meeting. In 1805, Dunn and his partner started a business that slid deeply into debt. He was disowned by the Meeting in 1816 because "he became embarrassed in his affairs and unable to meet his engagements."[68] Also, he had "assigned his effects so as to secure some of his creditors in preference to others."[69] Even after paying off his debt thirteen years later, he did not rejoin the Friends.

So, what does a man in dire financial straits do in 1818 to correct the situation? In Nathan Dunn's case, he went to China. The Chinese trade was a way to make up lost fortunes. How does one come up with the capital for this kind of venture? He borrowed the money and a ship from one of his creditors, who hoped that this would enable Dunn to repay his debt—and it worked.

Dunn set up a trading company in Canton, called Nathan Dunn & Company. As one of the few merchants who refused to trade in opium, he gained an honorable reputation with the Chinese government. His method of trading was different from most. Instead of only sending the usual teas, silks, porcelain and rice to Philadelphia and returning with an empty ship, he filled it with goods picked for the Chinese market, like silver coins, furs and ginseng. In some cases, he had items made specifically for the Chinese trade. His fortunes started growing rapidly.

Dunn spent the years in China limited to the twelve-acre section of Canton waterfront, where all the foreign traders or "barbarians" were located. The Qing government wanted to limit their contact with the general Chinese population. Ships were required to stop at Macao to obtain permission, or chop, to travel to Whampoa with their Chinese pilot. From there, the ships traveled up the Pearl River to Canton, where they were refitted and made to wait. Trade was controlled by the Co-Hong, a group of eight to ten wealthy Chinese merchants. This group sold the cargo, assessed the duties and took responsibility for the ships while they were in port.

Because of the amount of time spent waiting, Dunn started collecting Chinese items, but not the normal trade items. He had gained a very good reputation with the government because of his opposition to the opium trade. He was allowed to hire people who collected these treasures in areas of China that traders couldn't access. The things he collected crossed all aspects of Chinese life and culture, from the very rich to the very poor. Eventually, this collection became Dunn's Chinese Museum in Philadelphia and, later, in London. His collection listings from his tour guidebook for the exhibit "Ten Thousand Chinese Things" also gives some indication of what may have been in his garden in the way of structures. The architect who designed his house created the Chinese collection's museum in London, whose design was based on a summerhouse miniature Dunn had in the collection. Another item, a pagoda, purchased from Dunn's collection in 1842, spent a decade in one of the lakes at Victoria Park in London. Effects of neglect and war led to its eventual demolition. It is also probable that Dunn would have made some of his landscaping plans based on what he had seen and heard about while in China.

Two books, part of Dunn's library, document the development of what eventually became Dunn's Chinese Cottage. The books, *Designs for Rural Residences* and *Frendall's Designs for Cottages*, are currently housed in the Mount Holly Library, part of Dunn's collection left to the library upon his death. In both books, two men, Alexander Pope and Lancelot "Capability" Brown are frequently mentioned. I will try to pull together a short summary of why Dunn was interested in these gentlemen. Please bear with me as I digress a bit.

In the early eighteenth century, a landscape architect, Lancelot "Capability" Brown, started using more natural landscape designs very similar to what Dunn's property eventually looked like. Dunn may have visited some of the properties that Brown worked on in England—Stowe, Castle Howard and Stourhead. Capability Brown's landscapes tried to achieve the perfection of nature by using large-scale areas with hills, water, trees, mossy caverns and sham ruins known as garden follies to create a picture-perfect landscape. A boundary of woodland with small groups of trees farther in would be visible in the distance. Water elements were used boldly, with a clear meadow area.

Additional Brown landscape characteristics included curved and meandering lines. A series of "informal" vistas punctuated by focal points in the form of classical temples, ruins and benches were used. The garden would be open to the surrounding parkland, where it became part of the overall plan. Lastly, the plantings would consist of groupings of different sizes, shapes and colors for a balanced and focused sight line. Capability Brown swept formality aside.

Alexander Pope, a prominent poet of the early eighteenth century also focused on the naturalistic landscape movement, as noted in the poem at the start of this chapter. He had a following of several eighteenth-century gardens all based on his picturesque writing style. He believed that the architectural style of the house should complement the garden. Again, planting beds should be curved, not pointed, and irregularly shaped, with the beds cut out of the turf. Pope's own property, Twickenham, though small, like many

Above: 1. Mount Holly's bit of Williamsburg. This garden features vegetable gardening in a small space. *Courtesy of Nina Gee.*

Right: 2. Poppies blooming in the same Mount Holly garden. *Courtesy of Nina Gee.*

3. Visiting a coneflower, another U.S. native. *Photo taken at Reynolda Garden in Winston-Salem, North Carolina.*

4. Camas, native to Idaho and used as a food by the American Indians, blooms in author's backyard.

Right: 5. The former front doors of the Mount Holly Library as they may have looked before the community room was added. *Courtesy of Nina Gee.*

Below: 6. The Mount Holly Library from across the street. *Courtesy of Larry Tigar.*

7. The Saint Francis garden at Sacred Heart Church. *Courtesy of Larry Tigar.*

8. One of the many backyards in Mount Holly where specimen plants from former larger gardens still survive. *Courtesy of Larry Tigar.*

9. Sacred Heart Parish House. *Courtesy of Larry Tigar.*

10. A Japanese maple, also part of the Levis Garden. *Courtesy of Larry Tigar.*

Above: 11. A horse chestnut tree flower.

Left: 12. The fishpond with waterfall. The pond dates to the early 1900s and was part of Levis Garden, but the waterfall is a more recent addition. *Courtesy of Mark Doegnes*.

Above: 13. Roses in one of the
backyards showcased during the
Hidden Gardens Tour of Mount
Holly. *Courtesy of Larry Tigar.*

Right: 14. The Friends' meetinghouse
in early spring. The daffodils were
planted as part of a daffodil festival.
Courtesy of Nina Gee.

15. A small sampling from a garden on the 2007 Hidden Gardens Tour. *Courtesy of Nina Gee.*

The Chinese Cottage

16. A rendering of what Nathan Dunn's garden may have looked like. *Courtesy of Barbara Helmechi.*

of the properties he worked on for his friends, maintained these principals. In 1734, Pope stated that "all gardening is landscape painting. Just like a landscape hung up."[70]

After a big send-off in Canton, Dunn returned to Philadelphia. With his accumulated wealth, one of the first things he did was to host a dinner to which he invited all of his creditors. Under each plate was a check for the amount that he owed, plus interest. At the age of forty-two, Dunn retired from business to pursue the life of a gentleman in Jacksonian America.

After spending a number of years pursuing financial success, one could become a virtuous gentleman only by withdrawing from the business sphere, devoting one's time and energies to the public welfare, whether that involved entering politics, engaging in scientific pursuits, or assisting in worthy philanthropic causes.[71]

Dunn joined the American Philosophical Society and the Academy of Natural Sciences, became vice president of the Pennsylvania Institution for the Instruction of the Blind and was affiliated with many other organizations. He gave $20,000 to Haverford College, a Quaker institution in financial difficulties. He also became involved in the creation of Laurel Hill Cemetery, serving as chairman. This is also where Nathan Dunn met the man who would design "The Cottage" in Mount Holly.

In 1837, Dunn hired Notman to design his English cottage with an oriental flair, including the outbuildings. Notman was born in Edinburg, Scotland, in 1810. He studied at the Royal Academy of Scotland. In 1831, he immigrated to the United States, where he started his career as a carpenter. The Library Company of Philadelphia was Notman's first job as an architect. This is where he met John Jay Smith, who later introduced him to Dunn and another member, George Washington Doane.

What we know about the gardens of this property is limited. There is some information about the house and property layout based on an insurance description done in 1837. Dunn was very involved in the plans for his cottage. "The aim in designing it being something adapted to the American climate, in fitness and expression of purpose, rather than to follow any fixed style."[72] We do know that the following plantings existed, as noted in Leah Blackman's book, *History of Little Egg Harbor Township, Burlington County, N.J.*:

The trees he had planted have grown to noble specimens of their kind— looking as a century might have rolled away since they were planted; those magnificent Magnolia trees with their immense and beautiful blossoms are

Dunn's privy, now part of Sacred Heart Roman Catholic Church in Mount Holly.

almost too beautiful for this world; and the evergreens have spread themselves like "green bay trees."[73]

There are three other things we know about Dunn's property. The first is that he grew grapes. His gardener, William H. Carse, competed in what is now the Philadelphia Flower Show in 1843. An interesting feature of the Philadelphia Flower Show, even today, is how the competitors have to force the plants they are showing into bloom or fruit. Mr. Carse was showing "the finest forced grapes...St. Peters, White Muscat of Alexandria, Frankenthal, Constantia of Zante, and Black Hamburg. The whole of this contribution is splendid."[74] The White Muscat, a wine grape, and Black Hamburg, a table grape, are noted in Bernard McMahon's *American Gardener's Calendar* as grapes with good flavor that fruited plentifully.

It is mentioned in a letter in possession of a relative of Dunn's that he collected tree specimens from all over the world. At the time Dunn was collecting, plant exploration was in its infancy. Missionaries located in India, the West Indies, the Far East and Africa started as the network of collectors. Most combined their work with an avid interest in the local plant life. The United States contained many examples of highly collectible trees and shrubs. Plants from the Lewis and Clark expedition were now readily available. Because Dunn was involved in the export business, it is probable that he had plants shipped here from China and England. Overseas shipping of plants had started to improve about this time. Dunn belonged to several organizations, such as the American Philosophical Society, where it was likely that these prominent gentlemen would have traded specimens amongst themselves.

A man of Nathan Dunn's stature would have been able to purchase plants from all over the country at some of the best-known nurseries. Prince Nursery in Flushing, Long Island, New York, was one of the first nurseries to offer ornamentals for sale. It was established in 1732 as a seller of fruit trees. The D&C Landreth Nursery started in Philadelphia in 1784 as a seed house. Just across the Delaware River was Bartram's Nursery. Included among the Dunn papers, located in the Burlington County Lyceum of Natural Science and History in Mount Holly, is an article about William Bartram published in *The Cabinet of Natural History and Rural American Sports* in 1833. The nursery was in operation from 1783 to 1850 with, first, John Bartram Jr. overseeing it and then his granddaughter, Ann, and her husband, Richard Carr. Bartram's nursery was the first nursery to print a comprehensive catalogue of American plants.

Henry A. Dreer Inc., also located in Philadelphia, started as a seed house in 1838 on Chestnut Street. The company moved its seed-growing operation to "The Woodlands" greenhouses from 1839 to 1850 while maintaining the Chestnut Street office. The Woodlands, now a cemetery, was once the estate of William Hamilton, a contemporary of Thomas Jefferson. Hamilton was one of two people (the other being Bernard McMahon, also from Philadelphia) who grew the seeds and cuttings from the Lewis and Clark expedition. Dreer's later moved to Cinnaminson. It went out of business in 1943.

After Dunn died of malaria in Switzerland in 1842, he left the property, which also included a wharf lot located about two hundred yards from the house, to his sisters and their children to live in until they, too, passed away. His sister, Rhoda, lived there until 1881. The property was sold in November 1881 to Franklin Burr Levis, who is discussed in another chapter. Some of the money from the proceeds of the sale was to be used to start the Mount Holly Library. The house went through several owners, who updated it to the way it looks today. A second floor and third floor were added, along with other exterior changes. Eventually, the property was abandoned. It became a convent and school right after World War II. Classes were held in the house until it was outgrown and the current school was built. The stable was moved to High Street, where it became a double home. The other building that remains is the privy/bathhouse building, which is now a food pantry for St. Vincent DePaul.

Dunn's stable, converted to private homes.

As mentioned before, there are some who remember what was in Dunn's garden when they were children, either because they attended school there or they used the garden as a cut through. This oriental oasis still had running fountains and a pond. There were still some rosebushes. The greenhouse, which stocked the interior of the house with exotic plants, was torn down to make room for the school. The conservatory was removed, but the outline of the building remained until recently, with no one knowing what it was. The parking lot paved over what remained of the garden except for one sycamore still located in the middle of the asphalt. An auditorium was built behind the school. In the early 1990s, the new church was built to the right of the house. The pine trees along the front of the house are also original to the property. The brick wall was added sometime between 1885 and 1917. The current gardens are taken care of by volunteers.

Riverside and the Bishop

One in the house spoke one day, as she came up the garden, whose border is full of pansies all the year, of a purple cloud of hearts-ease. In five minutes he [Bishop Doane] *gave her this:*

"That cloud of hearts-ease dearest,
'Twas a most poetic thought,
And instant to my loving head,
Such prayer as this, it brought:
That clouds of hearts-ease, evermore,
And wheresoe'er thou art,
May pour their purple perfume down,
In blessings of thy heart."

George Washington Doane was born in Trenton in 1799. He could have followed any career path available, but he chose theology. In 1821, he was ordained a deacon in the Episcopal Church, becoming a priest in 1823. He married his wife, Eliza, who was a widow of a wealthy Bostonian, in 1829. Over the years, he rose steadily through the church to become the bishop of the New Jersey Diocese in 1832, a position he held until his death in 1859. In 1837, he founded Saint Mary's Hall for Girls, where he could combine his talents of being a prelate, a poet and an educator. Saint Mary's was the first effort in America "to educate the church's girls in the church's ways."[75] Both Saint Mary's and Burlington College for Boys and Men (founded in 1846) were financed by Doane and his wife.

Doane, like Dunn, met John Notman while part of the planning committee of Laurel Hill Cemetery. This project was the first time Notman was commissioned to design the landscape of a property, as well as the

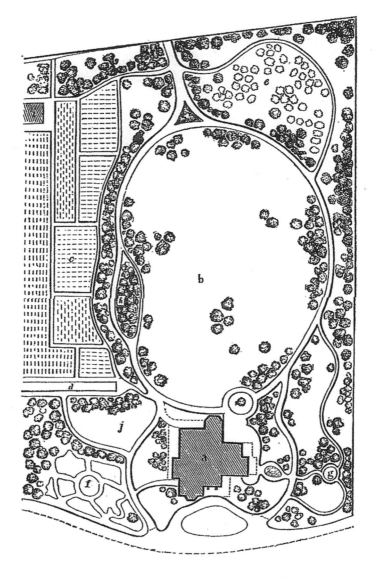

A landscaping map of Riverside from Downing's book, *A Treatise*.

house. Notman began "Riverside Villa" in 1837, with completion in 1839, when Doane, his wife and two sons moved in. The house and grounds, located along River Road in Burlington's most aristocratic area of town, was situated so that views of the Delaware River could be seen from the drawing room, hall and library through the diamond-paned windows. Additionally, the pleasure grounds could be seen from the opposite side of the house. Andrew Jackson Downing described these grounds as follows:

> *On one side of the area is the kitchen garden, c, separated and concealed from the lawn by thick groups of evergreens and deciduous trees. At c, is a picturesque orchard, in which the fruit trees are planted in groups, instead of straight lines, for the sake of effect.*[76]

He went on to describe the placement of the flower gardens under the windows. The walkway around the lawn was also the carriage road to get from the front of the property to the back, where the outbuildings were located. Riverside was noted as being the first and finest Italianate-style building in America. Unfortunately, in 1851, due to the economy and certain financial obligations related to the building costs, Doane had to sign over the

Doane's home, Riverside. *Courtesy of the Burlington County Historical Society.*

properties to a board of trustees; however, he did retain educational control of both Saint Mary's and Burlington College.

After the diocese divided in 1874, Riverside was slowly partitioned into classrooms. As the years passed, maintenance costs became an issue. Burlington College closed. Saint Mary's Hall still remains. An effort was made to save the house in 1961, but it was eventually demolished. One of the magnificent fireplace surrounds can be seen at the Burlington County Historical Society's Museum. Today, you can still walk along "Greenbank" of Burlington, where it can still be said that "between these old homesteads and the river is a picturesque driveway and walk guarded by tall elms and beyond is the gently flowing river."[77] An example of Notman's work, a small chapel, can be seen at Saint Mary's Doane Academy in Burlington.

The Cemetery as
a Garden

THE CEMETERY is his most fitting monument. His name will be associated with it, for generations to come, and many a denizen of the town, as he visits its refreshing shades, to seek relaxation from the cares of the world, or relief from the heat of Summer, will pause in silent and solemn deference, at the grave of him, to whom alone, his thanks are due, for this appropriate Place of Retirement, and who now sleeps beneath its sods.[78]

Why would cemeteries be included in a book about gardens? The simple answer is that, about 1831, a new movement began in this country—rural cemeteries. Land in cities was becoming hard to come by, and any open space was needed to build on. Earlier cemeteries were flat, with rows of gravestones surrounded by grass; sometimes they were so neglected that families could not find the markers of deceased loved ones. A.J. Downing, in his book *Rural Essays*, published after his death, wrote, "Twenty years ago, nothing better than a common grave-yard filled with high grass, and a chance sprinkling of weeds and thistles, was to be found in the Union."[79]

The rural cemetery movement in the United States started with Mount Auburn Cemetery in Boston, Massachusetts. The design idea for this cemetery came from Père Lachaise in Paris, now that country's most famous cemetery and largest park. Mount Auburn Cemetery was opened in 1804 on the outskirts of Boston to reduce the dreadful burial conditions in the city. It was designed by Jacob Bigelow and the Massachusetts Horticultural Society. The founders of Mount Auburn wanted to create a space that would be inspirational to the living. The concept of rural cemeteries was to incorporate a park-like setting with panoramic vistas outside the city and separate from the church. Mount Auburn became a popular nineteenth-century location for recreation and contemplation. Because of Mount Auburn, Laurel Hill

One of Philadelphia's lesser-known rural cemeteries, Woodlawn.

Cemetery in Philadelphia was developed, although the design was based on Kensal Green in London. According to Downing:

> *The three leading cities of the north, New-York, Philadelphia, Boston, here, each of them, besides their grand cemeteries,—Greenwood, Laurel Hill, Mount Auburn,—many others of less note; but say of which would have astonished and delighted their inhabitants twenty years ago.*[80]

What made a group of gentlemen from Philadelphia interested in this endeavor? The project organizer, John Jay Smith, a librarian at the Library Company, went to visit the grave site of his young daughter and found the cemetery in such deplorable condition that her resting place could not be located. Smith got together some prominent Philadelphians with whom he was acquainted and an architect, John Notman, who he knew from work at the Library Company, to start this new project.

Laurel Hill was started as a nondenominational cemetery located far enough from the city so as not encroach, but close enough so as not to be an obstacle when going at a funeral's pace to reach it. The park-like setting, filled with rare trees, a beautiful landscape and suitable soil, was meant as

A Legacy of the Landscape

A fine example of Mount Holly, showcasing the architecture and the garden. *Courtesy of Larry Tigar.*

much for the living as the dead. This rural cemetery followed the English picturesque landscape design. I'm going to let Andrew Jackson Downing explain why this was important:

> *More concisely, the Beautiful is nature or art obeying the universal laws of perfect existence (i.e. Beauty), easily, freely, harmoniously, and without the display of power. The Picturesque is nature or art obeying the same laws rudely, violently, irregularly and often displaying power only.*[81]

A large mansion was used in case of rain, with enough stable space for forty horses and carriages. A greenhouse was to be built so it could be filled with ornamentals as needed for summer decoration.

Work on the cemetery began in April 1836, with Notman receiving final payment in 1840. He did continue to design monuments over the next fifteen years. On at least two occasions, Dunn helped Laurel Hill resolve financial difficulties. In amongst Dunn's papers at the Mount Holly Library is a copy of Mount Auburn's bylaws inscribed to Nathan Dunn and Isaac Risdon Sr. by Mount Auburn's treasurer. A total of $100,000 was spent to develop this well-publicized location destined to become a public attraction—a place to promenade on a Sunday afternoon. To give an idea of how many people visited Laurel Hill in season, I will again refer to Downing:

> *We may mention that at Laurel Hill, four miles from Philadelphia, an account was kept of the number of visitors during last season; and the sum total, as we were told by one of the directors, was nearly 30,000 persons, who entered the gates between April and December, 1848.*[82]

Daniel Bowen wrote of Mount Auburn:

> *In such a pleasing spot, where the birds sing over the graves, and flowers and trees present their ever new verdure, the dreariness is lost; the utter oblivion that awaits the tenant of a confined graveyard is forgotten—death is here robbed of half its horror.*[83]

Isaac Risdon

Isaac Risdon was a Mount Holly native. He was born in April 1800 to a family who settled here in the early eighteenth century. He was one of seven children. In 1816, he went to Philadelphia to learn the trade of tailoring. At the age of nineteen, Risdon had earned enough money to buy back his indentureship and marry. Through his forty-year marriage, he had ten children. Risdon became quite accomplished at tailoring, going on to partner with his brother, William, and later his brother-in-law, in shops in Philadelphia at different times. Risdon retired to Mount Holly in 1837 and, with his brother, began speculating in real estate. Dr. Read offers an example: "This property was also purchased of Mr. Merritt by Isaac and William Risdon who erected several frame dwellings."[84]

Risdon purchased his home at 314 Garden Street in 1837, as well. The house on the property had been built in 1832. Plans of the grounds of the house, showing the locations of the house, the ornamental gardens around the house and the barnyard, with a chicken house, carriage house, corn crib, stable, orchard and wood house, are located at the Winterthur Library. There was also a vegetable garden located on the property. By 1838, the brothers had purchased thirty-two hundred acres from various owners to lay out streets, build houses and possibly start a cemetery. At this time, Mount Holly had two cemeteries, the Quaker cemetery at the Friends' meetinghouse and the St. Andrews Episcopal/Baptist Cemetery. Risdon thought there should be a burial ground available for people who were not of those faiths.

James Langstaff, James Hulme and Risdon organized the Mount Holly Cemetery in 1841, acting as the managers. The cemetery was incorporated the same year, starting with four acres of an eleven-acre plot near the bottom of the Mount. Risdon was the largest investor, getting $3 from every plot sold, until the total reached $2,000, to help with the expenses related to the cemetery. "The land was to be used 'for the interment of deceased human bodies and for no other purpose.'"[85] Dr. Zachariah Read described the cemetery in the following way:

Much taste has been displayed and a truly beautiful receptacle has been prepared for the dead, a place to rest for the body, and for serenity and meditation…in the cities in particularly they have inaugurated the plan of selecting the most romantic situations, and far from the noise and bussle [sic] of the town…In the year 1841 this beautiful spot was solemnly set apart and dedicated by appropriate ceremonies as a home for the dead.[86]

A house-chapel, which is still standing today, was also built on the property. The first burial occurred on April 20, 1841.

Because Risdon became overextended financially, he returned to work as a tailor in Philadelphia in 1847. He worked there for a few years before setting up a shop in Mount Holly, where he continued to work until 1857, when he retired for the final time. Throughout this time, he acted as the sole manager and owner of the cemetery, until his death in 1860. After that, his brother, William, and son, Henry, operated the cemetery jointly. The following are some parting words from Risdon's obituary:

He naturally cherished a commendable pride in that interesting spot, "The Cemetery",—to the laying out and beautifying of which, he had devoted so much time, labor and expense. It was his delight, in pleasant weather, to visit it at early dawn, and have his mind refreshed and spirits enlivened by the morning song of the birds, as they perched upon the trees his own hands had planted. He never wearied of conducting visitors about the grounds, directing their attention to points of interest, explaining the nature

Mount Holly Cemetary, showing the cedar-lined drive to the gate.

Another tree-lined drive in Mount Holly Cemetary.

and habits of various trees, and detailing any little history that might be connected with either of them.[87]

The Mount Holly Cemetery has been added to over the years. In 1886 and 1887, clippings from the *Cowgill Scrapbook* note at least two additions. The importance of the aesthetics of the cemetery is mentioned in both. The two acres added in 1886 were to include "a clump of trees which will be allowed to stand, and benches will be put under them, and a large oak tree on the west side will not be disturbed."[88] An additional entrance gate was added at this time. The view from the knoll at the base of the Mount was extolled in the 1887 clipping: "Go up there and stand upon it and you will be convinced."[89] The cemetery is still in use today, and one can go there to admire the view, hear the birds sing and appreciate the mature trees just as Risdon did.

The Others

I have often thought that if heaven had given me choice of my position and calling, it should have been on a rich spot of earth, well watered, and near a good market for the productions of the garden. No occupation is so delightful to me as the culture of the earth, & no culture comparable to that of the garden...I am still devoted to the garden. But tho' an old man, I am but a young gardener.
—Thomas Jefferson to Charles Wilson Peale, Poplar Forest, August 20, 1811

In the introduction, I noted Mount Holly's rich horticultural and agricultural past. Mount Holly was also a popular summer retreat for Philadelphians, with the creek providing fishing and boating entertainment. One, especially one familiar with local history, will note the last names of these gardeners, here and throughout the book. Many residents still living here have the same last names. It was a very hard decision to choose who would be included in this book. Several of the gardens need further research, but I will do the best I can with what is available to me at this time. Because there is only so much space allowed and, shockingly, several other gardens and gardeners who should be mentioned, I will note them here with any descriptions found.

THE MOUNT

The first garden I will mention is not necessarily a garden. I am speaking of the Mount. The holly-covered Mount is where Mount Holly originally received its name. It is 185 feet above sea level, one of the highest points in Burlington County. In 1955, Henry Shinn described it as follows: "The virgin forest covering the Mount, traversed by a few Indian trails and untouched by the axe of the white settler, remained in almost primeval condition until 1829."[90] On two different occasions, the Mount was occupied by the British during the Revolutionary War. The first time was in December 1776, when the town was under the control of Hessian mercenaries whose cannons were stationed on the summit. The American troops engaged them from Iron Works Hill, hence the battle's name: the Battle of Iron Works Hill. The two spent the day volleying cannonballs back and forth before the Continentals moved on. The second time was in June 1778, when Sir Henry Clinton evacuated Philadelphia and spent two days on the Mount. Isaac Hazelhurst was the owner of the Mount at this time, having purchased it from the Cripps family, the original owners.

During Hazelhurst's ownership, he caused some controversy by selling timber to a local merchant for $1,000. Shinn referenced the following in his *Mount Holly Herald* article in 1955: "As a result the Mount was cut over and all the ancient trees destroyed."[91] Read pointed out that "time has again covered the hill with sturdy growth."[92] While Hazelhurst owned the property, it encompassed a large amount of acreage, but gradually, over time and with each subsequent owner, the amount of surrounding property decreased to what it is today.

Reverend Isaac Brown purchased the Mount and sold much of the acreage. He, along with several others, incorporated the Mount Observatory Company, which planned to put a telescope on the summit. The project was abandoned when Brown sold the property to another man, who planned on building a house on top of it. When that man died, it was sold again to someone who, according to rumor, was going to cut down and sell all the timber, repeating Hazelhurst's earlier actions. According to Shinn, "Public sentiment was aroused and attempts made to obtain funds to purchase the property and preserve it as a town park."[93] Through the efforts of the Business Men's Association, the Mount was purchased. Shinn noted that

> the deed prohibits the township selling the Mount or any part thereof, or to do or permit any act whereby any of the natural resources, living trees, sand, gravel, minerals or earth, may be removed or otherwise disturbed.[94]

The Mount was neglected for many years until 1934, when its cleanup was accepted as a project for the Civil Works Administration. In a few short weeks, it was cleared of the invasive vegetation, fallen trees and debris. Again, several members of the Business Men's Association contributed money and materials for the project. Mount Park was now open. In 1935, it received the addition of an altar to be used for Easter Sunrise Services by the Protestant

Churches of Mount Holly. In 1939, the Mount was recorded as Mount Holly Park, with a notation of "good path to the summit."[95] I will again use Shinn's words to describe the Mount:

> *Few communities can boast of owning such a charming unspoiled woodland haven and bird sanctuary so conveniently located…to preserve the quiet atmosphere of this place of spiritual solace where the worries of daily life can be laid aside and forgotten for a time and strength renewed. The peace of God that passeth all understanding rests upon the altar and it surroundings. It should not be disturbed.*[96]

BARTRAM'S OAK

I am digressing from the main subject of this chapter, but I felt this was an important enough bit to share in this section. After attending a short talk about the historic homes in Mount Holly in which the speaker mentioned a stand of Bartram oak trees where he played as a child, I decided to find more information about this tree variety. I contacted Bartram's Garden in Philadelphia, and its curator, Joel Fry, kindly got back to me. This variety of tree is a naturally occurring hybrid of the willow oak and the red oak known as *Quercus x heterophylla*. John Bartram was the first to observe these trees, possibly near his farm along the Schuylkill River in the 1740s. More clusters were later found. Mr. Fry notes a reference from "Notes on the Bartram Oak (*Quercus heterohylla*)" in *Proceedings of the Academy of Natural Sciences of Philadelphia* (1861) that states that the location of Mount Holly's cluster is by the train depot in Mount Holly.[97] Mount Holly does have a street named Bartram, but after inquiring about it, no one seems able to tell me if it was named for the trees or for the Bartram family who lived in town.

CHARLES BISPHAM'S GARDEN ESTATE

The Bispham family was another longtime Mount Holly family who arrived in the United States in 1734. The particular Bispham, whose garden I will discuss, was named Charles. He was born in 1798. His father died when he was thirteen, so he was sent to school in Philadelphia, where his upbringing was supervised by his older brother, who was part of the banking and overseas trading industry. After traveling extensively in his youth, Charles Bispham was able to return to his hometown and retire "from that time

A natural hybrid, the Bartram's Oak. There once was a stand of them by the Dunn property. This photo was taken in Bartram's Garden in Philadelphia.

until the day of his death devoting himself assiduously to the interests of the town, engaging actively in building improvements, farming, and other occupations."[98] He married in 1845 and had several children.

During his retirement years, "Mr. Bispham's time was passed in looking after his farms, in building and in the improvement of his estate."[99] His estate consisted of a schoolhouse, where his children were schooled by a private tutor. This was accessible by a bridge over the creek known as "Bispham's Bridge," whose wonderful scenery was available in stereoscopic views. Dr. Read described the Bispham property as follows: "All this property has lately been improved and beautified by Mr. Charles Bispham, which renders it one of the most beautiful residences in the county."[100] Its garden extended from Washington Street, one of the most fashionable streets in town at the time, all the way back to the creek. Shinn also noted a fountain on the property: "An attractive fountain near the Union Firehouse site was supplied with water piped from a spring in the high bank of Water Street, and other pipes conveyed the water to the Bispham home."[101]

Mr. Bispham greatly added to the comfort and convenience of the "homestead", making it a very attractive home. It is situated in a park-like enclosure, in which are many noble trees, and through which the Rancocas Creek or River, flows. [102]

Bispham was very involved in town. It is mentioned he would purchase rundown properties and improve or remove them, whichever was needed.

The appearance of the town was greatly improved by Bispham's life-long habit of buying old and dilapidated houses and rebuilding them, or leveling the lots and planting grass, which was always kept mowed. [103]

I will close this segment with the following note to the editor of the *New Jersey Mirror*, written in 1858:

The original lowly town, clustered its small houses in their vicinity:—and from the same cause the first Church (long since down,) was situated nearest to the Iron Works—where is now the first and oldest Grave Ground beyond the Creek. Charles Bispham, Esq., has been the greatest modern improver of the place. Witness his own mansion, so tastefully enlarged, from the primitive Forefathers' home, by the Creek side;—and his great improvement of the waste of Pine Land, beyond the Creek; also, the redemption of the swampy lands, which intervene, in the now meadow lands, bordering along the Creek. [104]

Fountain Square

Like every colonial town, Mount Holly had its market square in or close to the center of town. And like every good early colonial town, this was where the stocks and whipping post were located. These were eventually replaced by a maypole, followed by a flagpole installed in 1864, as observed by Joseph Cowgill in his scrapbook in 1878:

> *The remnant of the broken flag-staff at Market Place was taken down on Wednesday last, and the space is now clear. It is proposed to improve the spot in a permanent manner by enclosing a grass plot with a drinking fountain.*[105]

The flagpole was recycled into boards. Another clipping noted that the flagpole was originally the mast of a ship.

That same year, it was decided to purchase a fountain to be installed in the same spot. "A motion was adopted declaring it to be the judgment of those present that a suitable fountain should be procured and placed at Market Place."[106] The fountain was purchased from Robert Wood & Co. "The fountain itself, for which $250 was paid, is a $750 fountain."[107] It was supposedly from the World Exposition held in Philadelphia. It was iron,

Fountain 1. *Courtesy of Larry Tigar.*

with swans spouting water from their uplifted heads and Hebe (pronounced e-ve), the goddess of youth and cupbearer to the gods, perched on top, running with her pitcher in hand. The fountain settled into the center of the square, which became known as Fountain Square, where three of the busiest streets—High, Mill and Washington—all intersect. The fountain featured three tiers, one for people, one for horses and one for dogs.

Shinn noted that the fountain became a problem once cars became popular, forcing its removal. There is another humorous story of Hebe's demise. It seems that, because of the condition of the fountain and its years in the elements, Hebe "fell" for the gentleman who was decorating for the holidays. The fountain could not be repaired; it was removed and replaced with a traffic kiosk in 1922. Fast forward to 1988, when the Mount Holly Historical Society installed a new fountain based on the old design. The current fountain is of a smaller scale and is no longer in the middle of the intersection. Its place of honor is located along the side of the former Union Bank, now the Burlington County College Mount Holly Center, on the corner. It sits proudly, as one of Mount Holly's lovely features, surrounded by landscaping and benches where one can take a short respite and listen to the fountain's relaxing sounds. This spot is still known as Fountain Square today.

J. Wardell Brown's Garden Estate

It is hard to believe that Broad Street was once part of a larger property owned by John Wardell Brown, another family with deep roots in Mount Holly. My neighborhood sits on land where the chicken house, the icehouse or the orchard once stood. (I prefer to think the orchard was here.) This neighborhood wasn't built until after the 1890s. The street was here, running all the way through as it is today, as were the alleys located behind the houses that connect this whole area to downtown.

J. Wardell Brown, an attorney, and his brother inherited the property from their father. His brother died leaving no will, so Brown inherited everything. According to Dr. Read, "John Wardell Brown erected his spacious, elegant and costly edifice, costing, it is said about $25,000."[108] We also know that there was a fountain located in his yard based on the following description: "the J. Wardell Brown fountain at Broad and High Streets with its statue of Neptune, which stood for many years in a yard on West Washington Street, with the arm and hand grasping a trident broken off."[109] In a clipping dated June 4, 1875, from the *Cowgill Scrapbook*, Brown hosted a fundraising event, an evening of musical entertainment, in his parlor, where all the "best citizens, handsomely attired" were in attendance. The house was later purchased by Judge Benjamin H. Lee. Upon his death in 1901, the house became the Moose Lodge. It was torn down in the 1920s. A lasting reminder of the property is the stone wall edging the brick sidewalk along the first half of Broad and High Streets.

Broad Street is noted on older maps of Mount Holly as Broadway. As mentioned before, the street was laid out much earlier than the houses were built. The intention of the streetscape was to make it one of the most beautiful streets in town once it was developed. Broad Street was meant to connect the Risdon properties farther down, using a similar street system layout that had been implemented in Philadelphia. After Brown's death in 1886, the property, not the house, which had been previously sold, was inherited by his nieces and a nephew. Houses started springing up along the street in 1890. If one visits the first block of Broad Street, she will note three houses that are identical in construction. All three were built in 1890; two of them were owned by Brown family members, as was an additional one. I do think Broad Street is one of the most beautiful streets in Mount Holly.

MARGARET MORRIS

Margaret Morris was from Burlington. She lived on Wood Street with her four children, moving from Philadelphia after her husband's untimely death. She had to be dependent on family charity, something she found very hard to do, and lived with her sister and brother-in-law. One way she tried to become independent was to have an extensive garden where she could grow food for her family, as well as items to trade or sell. She was also skilled in the art of healing, so part of her garden was dedicated to herbs and plants to help with this. After living in Burlington for four years, she moved back to Philadelphia to be closer to her newly married son. Following the yellow fever epidemic in 1793, she and her five orphaned grandchildren moved back to Burlington, where she still had some family. During these years, she wrote a kind of gardening journal that gives a very good report of some of the day-to-day importance of having a garden between 1804 and 1809.[110]

A Destination Location

In fact, Mount Holly is a garden town; it has been so since the days of the first settlers.[111]

LEVIS GARDEN

I would like to start this chapter with the story of how I was introduced to Levis Garden. One day, while working at a local antiques shop, a man stopped by asking for directions to "The Gardens." As a new resident of the community, the only spot in town I knew of with this name was a rather disheveled neighborhood of townhouses that were once used as military housing when the local bases were fully operational. He insisted this wasn't the area he was looking for. The gardens were full of tulips, daffodils and azaleas, he said, you know, a garden. Vaguely, I recalled a photo I had seen in a book of an arbor standing in a garden that no longer existed, Levis Garden. He went on to tell me about childhood trips to the garden in early spring, right around Easter, when the daffodils and tulips were in full bloom, followed by the azaleas, rhododendrons and dogwoods and the fall chrysanthemum show closing out the season. The garden was a constant joy to local residents. Levis Garden was said to rival Longwood Gardens in Kennett Square, Pennsylvania, in its prime.

Now, I will continue the story of the Nathan Dunn estate and introduce the Levis family, so again, I must wander a bit before I get to the point. The Levis family was of French descent, another family with a rich history in the town. The first reference I find to the family is Samuel Levis, who is listed as owning a paper mill in 1856. He also owned property on Mill Street. His son, Franklin Burr Levis, is where we will begin.

Mrs. Franklin Burr Levis. *Courtesy of the Mount Holly Historical Society.*

Franklin Burr Levis was born in 1834. He went to the Mount Holly schools until he was fourteen, at which time he was sent to a boarding school. He attended Haverford College and, later, Princeton. He was an attorney, admitted to the bar in 1856. He married Rebecca Coppuck in 1857. Together, they had three sons, Howard, Edward and Norman. Mr. Levis was involved with several corporations in town, as well as several civic organizations. He housed the Burlington County Lyceum of Natural Sciences and History in his downtown building starting in 1859.

As I mentioned earlier, Nathan Dunn left his estate to his sisters, Phebe and Rhoda, to live in for the rest of their lives. After their deaths, Phebe in 1855 and Rhoda in 1880, the property was to be sold with a portion of the proceeds to go toward a library, as reflected in the following statement from Dunn's will:

> ...*and to apply the interest and income of such investments from time to time in the purchase of books and in forming a useful library to be opened in some appropriate and well-selected institution in or near Mount Holly, to be kept open during such hours and times as may be most convenient and useful for the persons for whose use it is designated. It is my will that the said library may be devoted to the use of persons residing in and about Mount Holly generally and more practically to the use and benefit of young men and apprentices.*[112]

Under the Japanese maple. *Courtesy of Mark Doegnes.*

The Chinese Cottage and its property were sold at auction on January 12, 1881, with Franklin Burr Levis purchasing it. As stipulated in Dunn's will, the proceeds, $10,600, went to the Burlington County Lyceum to start up the Mount Holly Library. Heirs of Dunn's estate did try to contest the will, but the courts found in favor of the lyceum.

Levis made extensive changes to the house, renaming it Dunmore. It went from a Chinese Cottage to a Colonial Revival style. The house's octagonal windows were replaced by bay windows. Brick replaced the wooden shakes on the first floor. The second half story was expanded to a full story, and eventually a third floor was added. The front porch underwent changes as well, going from across the front to over the door, with large, circular columns reminiscent of the plantation homes in the South, where the Levises had extended family. This is where their three sons were raised. Their middle son, Edward, will be discussed further in this chapter. Mr. Levis's brother built a house farther down the street in 1887, as noted in the *Cowgill Scrapbook*.

After Mr. Levis's death in 1913, Dunmore was sold to John and Elizabeth Johnson Sr. They also made changes to the house.

> *When Mr. Johnson purchased it, some years later, he made many additions and improvements, and "Dunmore" became the center of much social life. Mrs. Johnson, beautiful and charming, was a gracious and popular hostess, and when the family moved to Philadelphia, there was much regret in Mount Holly.*[113]

The home was also owned by James Mercer Davis and his family. As time passed, the house and grounds went through several other owners who all found the property too expensive to keep up. It was saved by the township when an owner decided he wanted to divide it into apartments. This was something common in town during the early to mid-1940s. The township was interested in making the building a community center, but it was considered too unsafe. The house sat empty for a number of years. After World War II, nuns from the Immaculate Heart of Mary purchased the building to use as a convent and school.[114] Eventually, the garden was taken over by new buildings and parking lots. The stable was moved across the street and is now a double house. The privy/bathhouse is now occupied by Saint Vincent de Paul's food pantry. The house and property are all part of the Parish of Sacred Heart.

Edward Hulme Levis was the middle son of Franklin Burr and Rebecca Levis. His older brother, Howard, was a lawyer for General Electric in

Eleanor at the front of Johnson's house, formerly Dunn's Cottage. *Courtesy of Eleanor Rich.*

London, while his younger brother, Norman, was a rector at the Church of the Incarnation in Philadelphia. Edward worked in the banking and brokerage industry in New York for many years before his retirement in 1929. He married and settled into the home formerly belonging to his uncle Howard. The *Cowgill Scrapbook* notes, "George Branin has just completed Howard Levis' residence on Main street. It is one of the finest houses in Mount Holly."[115] After Levis took up residence there, he began to create a

Eleanor's sister, Dorothy, standing on the front lawn of the Johnson house. *Courtesy of Eleanor Rich.*

Sacred Heart front porch. *Courtesy of Larry Tigar.*

A locust tree flower. The tree was once part of Levis Garden.

new garden, one for which Mount Holly would become known. In 1916, he placed a help-wanted ad in the *New Jersey Mirror* looking for a gardener with "a thorough knowledge of flowers."[116]

I had seen pictures and slides of this garden. People have told me stories about it—how their parents would take them there during Easter and photograph them among the blooming tulips and daffodils. The same happened with weddings. There are even a few plant specimens and some garden architectural pieces in existence where backyards now line the borders of what was Levis Garden. It wasn't until Eleanor Rich from the Mount Holly Historical Society shared a family movie with me that I grasped what the man asking for "The Garden" at the antique store was talking about. The beauty of Levis Garden was breathtaking. I hope I can do it the justice it deserves with the following description and pictures.

I am unsure when Levis started his garden, but I've been told that it was in the early 1900s. In one of the backyards, there is a fishpond whose occupants are descendants of those fish put there by Mr. Levis. The pond is located with a Japanese maple and a horse chestnut tree from his garden. There is also some trelliswork very similar to a photograph of a garden in another

A Legacy of the Landscape

Under the horse chestnut tree. *Courtesy of Mark Doegnes.*

yard taken in 1924 and displayed at the Archives of American Gardens in the Smithsonian. The garden

> *covers more than five acres. A large part of the garden follows a formal design and possesses balance, dignity and charm. The pergolas are well placed, vineclad and enticing. Here one may rest and look out across the spreading lawns to the beautiful trees of the bird sanctuary. The subtle informality of the estate is a masterly transition from the well-tended garden to the natural woodland, a detail that is too often overlooked in the fettered making of gardens.*[117]

There was also a bird sanctuary in the garden. This explains three structures I've seen in pictures that I thought were enclosed twig gazebos, but I could never see an entrance. These structures were probably giant cages to house some of the birds.

Mr. Levis was a member of the American Rose Society, the American Peony Society and the Mount Holly Garden Club. He was also very active in his church. He helped to preserve the Mount in 1934 by contributing money

Walking through Levis Garden. *Courtesy of Burlington County Historical Society.*

A Levis Garden postcard. *Courtesy of the Mount Holly Historical Society.*

The fishpond from Levis Garden behind one of the homes on the Mount Holly Garden Tour. *Courtesy of Larry Tigar.*

and materials toward the project and serving on the commission. He was mentioned again in the *New Jersey Mirror* when he dedicated a pin oak tree to a recently deceased member of the Mount Holly Garden Club in 1938. Mr. Levis died in December 1939 in an automobile accident. His will stipulated a wish to keep the garden going, and he did leave an income to do this, but at some point the money ran out. Two things happened about this same time: Mount Holly needed a school, and the garden was too expensive and hard to maintain. On what used to be Levis Garden now sits Holbein Middle School. I was told by people who watched the gardens being dug up that there must have been forty thousand to fifty thousand bulbs in areas. Even now, in the spring, one can find an escapee from the bulb garden in amongst the wooded area on the side of the school. Levis Garden is remembered fondly by those who had the privilege to see it.

Snippets

While New Jersey is the thirty-fifth state in size, she is the nineteenth in population, twenty-fifth in value of agricultural products, sixth in products of manufacture, seventh in products of mines, eighth in valuation of real and personal property, first in means of communication by railroads and first in the valuation of farm land per acre. Burlington county is second in agricultural products in the United States, Lancaster, Pa., being first, owing to its enormous crops of tobacco.[118]

This next section includes gardening bits and pieces I have found that I felt merit mentioning. The first person I will introduce is Josiah White. He built one of the first fulling (the process of cleaning wool and then thickening it by matting the fibers together) mills in the area. His grandfather was an original passenger on board the *Kent* when it arrived. White moved to Mount Holly in 1730 after purchasing one hundred acres along the creek, where he built his mill and home. Like many in the area, he was a member of the Society of Friends, and like John Woolman, who arrived in town ten years later, he was an abolitionist. DeCou wrote the following about White: "He was skilled in the use of herbs and ointments, in the treatment of disease and invariably declined to accept pay for his services, as he felt his skill was a gift of God."[119] White used his skills to help treat the sick and wounded during the Hessian occupation of Mount Holly in December 1776. White died in 1780, but his mill lasted until 1881, when it was destroyed by a fire. The house, large and brick, was torn down in 1885.

Gardens, like people, go through cycles, averaging about twenty years each. This next set of gardens are for the most part from the 1930s. Misses Mary and Emma Etris lived on Garden Street. The house on the property was built in 1775 and still retains much of its originality. The garden is mentioned in two locations. The first is in a set of typewritten papers from 1973 at the Mount Holly Historical Society when the town was applying to become a historic district with the National Trust for Historic Preservation. The last line of the description reads: "The garden in the rear of the property is known for its privacy, selection of wild flowers, and an extensive collection of shrubs and trees."[120] The privacy is mentioned again by John T. Faris: "You forget the present, with all its hurry and confusion. Here is a place in which you want to linger."[121] In this backyard, there were box-edged flower beds, wisteria-clad trellises and a small rock garden–edged pond, plus an assortment of trees and shrubs.

Miss Sara Leeds lived on Branch Street, across from the Woolman Memorial. Her garden is also noted in the Faris book as having large quantities of boxwood, "which rivals in number and perfection of the individual plants the boxwood of the most famous gardens in Virginia."[122] Leeds was the founder of the Mount Holly Garden Club, which is still in existence today. She started the club in 1927. By 1931, Faris wrote: "Included among its

The former home of Edward B. Jones.

members a number whose homes are surrounded by beautiful old gardens. Miss Sara Leeds was the enthusiast who persuaded ninety of her neighbors to enter the organization."[123] The Mount Holly Garden Club is the oldest garden club in Burlington County. I am sure Miss Leeds would be thrilled to know it is still around.

Among the High Street gardens I will note this one, owned by Edward B. Jones, a director of the Burlington County Railroad Company. His garden, located behind his house, met up with what was once Dunn's garden. Faris noted the Jones garden as having many unusual specimens of trees and shrubs.

> *The "Lazy Garden" occupying the open sunny part of the grounds lends a colorful bit of highlight to the garden. Here, without rhyme or reason, Mr. Jones each year broadcasts a quantity of seeds of both annuals and perennials which are afterward left to take care of themselves.*[124]

The Jones garden. *Courtesy of Mount Holly Historical Society.*

One item of interest I noted when studying photos of this garden is the placement of palm trees throughout. Some are in pots, but some are in the ground, making me wonder if there wasn't a greenhouse or conservatory on the property, as well.

Next, I will turn to some of the nurseries from the area. Thus far, I've been able to find references to three. The first reference is an ad for grape vines, which I found in the *Cowgill Scrapbook*. The ad is dated October 26, 1864, and mentions "GRAPE VINES in all their varieties, together with Blackberry, Raspberry and Strawberry Plants, to which he calls the attention of the public."[125] This nursery was located on the then-outskirts of town, past the Dunn and Langstaff estates, close to where the Mount is located. Another nursery was called Evergreen Avenue Nursery. According to the return address, it sold strawberry plants and peach trees. Unfortunately, this is the only reference I could find about this business, and the next one, as well. Woodlane Nursery was located even farther outside of town than the first nursery I mentioned. According to the letterhead, Woodlane started in 1837. The inside letter was an order for privet hedges, one of the nursery's specialties, from Lancaster County Nurseries, a supplier in Lancaster, Pennsylvania, in 1910. The last name of the owner was Rogers. I bought the two envelopes on, of all places, eBay. The final reference, found in the *New Jersey Mirror*, is about C.B. Neale, who sent some of his "choice plants" over to London for the 1851 World's Fair. This is all the information I have found on local nurseries so far, but the hunt is not over.

A letter from Evergreen Nurseries.

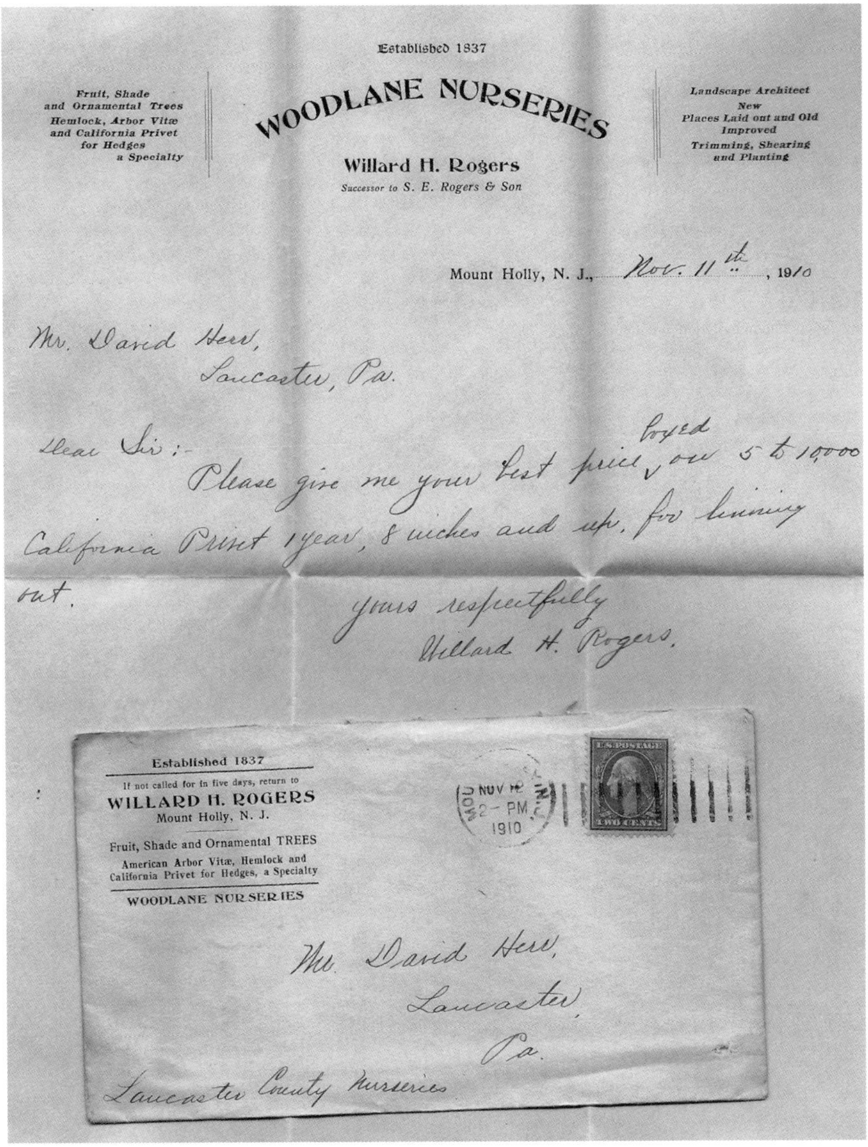

Established 1837

Fruit, Shade and Ornamental Trees Hemlock, Arbor Vitæ and California Privet for Hedges a Specialty

WOODLANE NURSERIES

Willard H. Rogers

Successor to S. E. Rogers & Son

Landscape Architect New Places Laid out and Old Improved Trimming, Shearing and Planting

Mount Holly, N. J., Nov. 11th, 1910

Mr. David Herr,
Lancaster, Pa.

Dear Sir:-
Please give me your best price, boxed, on 5 to 10,000 California Privet 1 year, 8 inches and up, for lining out.

Yours respectfully
Willard H. Rogers.

Established 1837
If not called for in five days, return to
WILLARD H. ROGERS
Mount Holly, N. J.
Fruit, Shade and Ornamental TREES
American Arbor Vitæ, Hemlock and California Privet for Hedges, a Specialty
WOODLANE NURSERIES

NOV 2-PM 1910

U.S. POSTAGE TWO CENTS

Mr. David Herr,
Lancaster,
Pa.
Lancaster County Nurseries

A note from Woodlane Nurseries.

Being close to the creek, Mount Holly had a lot of manufacturing going on besides the mills. In the *Cowgill Scrapbook* there is a September 1882 clipping about a building that had recently changed hands. It went from being a cannery to a creamery to a match factory. There was good news about the change, however: "finding difficulty in getting the required help at all times, will remove to Mt. Holly, thus adding another industry to give employment to our people."[126] When this building was a cannery, it was owned by Abraham Anderson. I found a reference from a book, *Fresh Tastes from the Garden State*, about Mr. Abraham partnering up with a soup manufacturer in 1869 to start Campbell's Soup. The Eagle Foundry Company sent a plough to the World's Fair in London in 1851. This was the first World's Fair where the Crystal Palace was in the news, showing all the latest innovations from all over the world.

Speaking of fairs, the county fair was always a big deal growing up in Nebraska. It was where everyone got together to show off their farm animals, preserves and baked goods, plus all kinds of miscellaneous items, while having fun on the midway and eating way too much sugary food. It's been nice to see the same enjoyment of the farm when I came here to New Jersey. The Mount Holly Fair started in October 1847. Until 1856, the fair bounced around to various locations before finding its permanent home on the other side of the Mount. A racetrack, grandstands and exhibition buildings were added to the location. A bigger, more ornate grandstand was built in 1887, when the racetrack became a popular spot in the area to watch the trotters and the pacers. By 1939, there were a few auto races still, but for the most part it was no longer used. The fair was disbanded in 1926, and the grounds were sold in 1955 to a developer. The shopping center that is now there is known as Fairgrounds Plaza. The Burlington County Farm Fair has moved to another town a few miles away, but it is still very reminiscent of county fairs of the past. We also have a mural depicting the Mount Holly Fair on one of our downtown buildings.

I hope these snippets have shown a little about the agricultural and horticultural history of Mount Holly. In many cases, gardens and gardening were part of daily life and it is often difficult to find written information—it just wasn't written down. As I research the town, I continually find more items, more of those "snippets" that could lead to something bigger over the passage of time.

Pests and Pestilence

There is nothing more important at this season, than the destruction of weeds, in all parts of the nursery, for if you let any of them perfect seeds, your ground will be thereby, stocked for years; therefore, the hoe must be applied wherever you can use it.[127]
—Bernard McMahon, The American Gardener's Calendar, *1806*

I begin this chapter with a story—the story of a plant, native to the United States and sent to Sweden in 1753. The battle with the *Toxicodendron radicans* continues today. It has been there for a long time, in a lined hole with brick edging and a small fence. Continual trimming tries to keep it under control. It's hard to believe, knowing sensitive people can break out in a red itchy rash that spreads all over the body, that this plant was once considered highly collectible. Some don't even need to touch it; the wind carries the toxins. Others are so sensitive that they require immediate medical treatment. A sample was sent to Carl Linnaeus. He gave it the Greek name *rhus* for sumac, which was changed to *Toxicodendron*, meaning "poison-tree," *radicans*, meaning "rooting." Does it sound familiar? Maybe this rhyme will help: "leaves of three let them be." Poison ivy was once considered an exotic plant, much prized in the European horticultural circles. It needed to be named, so a sample was sent to Linnaeus in Sweden, and the plant is still there. Talk about longevity!

A weed by definition is an unwanted plant growing where it is not wanted. The definition is also open to interpretation; a weed might not always be a weed to some, or it might be a weed in one space but not a weed in another. For example, for some, the black-eyed Susan currently growing in my vegetable garden would be considered a weed. However, I think of it as misplaced. Once it is done flowering, I will dig it up and put it in its proper location with the other prairie plants. Until then, the tomatoes and green beans will just have to put up with it. The tomato volunteers growing in the same area I do consider weeds. Yes, I did keep some, but the other fifty or sixty just had to go. It's the interpretation. Several of our now-commonplace weeds and insects might have had a purpose at one time. A lot of them were introduced to this country. America had its own weeds, diseases and pests, of course, but over time and with immigration, these were added to. I'd like to give a brief history of some new and old ones.

Let's start with crabgrass. This common grass-like weed was brought here to be used for cattle pastures. "One admirer wrote in an agricultural periodical of 1820 that his pasture-sown crabgrass had 'as bright a color as I would ever desire on my plantation.'"[128] Of the twenty worst weeds of the early nineteenth century, compiled by Monticello's Center for Historic Plants, fourteen of them were introduced. In that time period, the controls were mainly of a biological nature, like hoeing and hand pulling. Jefferson's son-in-law found that if he let sheep graze in a field of thistle while it was young and just starting to flower, the sheep might not eat the leaves but would eat the flower, thereby reducing the plant's reproductive capabilities. Another method of weed control, which did help with insects, was to burn the field before planting. Overplanting an area was also a recommendation. To go with this one, it was suggested in the 1823 *American Farmer*, an agricultural periodical, to plant potatoes underneath fruit trees in the kitchen garden for two reasons: one, to break up the soil underneath, allowing for nutrients and water to penetrate, and two, to control weeds.

Fast forward to the Victorian era, when plants from all over the world were arriving in the United States, because of their collectability and marketability, to be used as ornamentals in yards and gardens everywhere. Because there weren't importation controls, or even much knowledge about growth habits, several exotic and now-threatening species were introduced. Among common escapees we still find today are Chinese wisteria, Japanese knotweed, kudzu and Japanese honeysuckle. Here, in Mount Holly, Chinese wisteria and Japanese knotweed are comfortably growing along the banks of the Rancocas Creek. The wisteria has killed trees because of its aggressive growth habits. Kudzu was grown as an ornamental vine before it escaped. It also likes to latch onto things and climb things. Once, my youngest son and I were clearing an area for planting, and he asked me about kudzu. I explained the whole thing to him, and he put an end to our conversation by remarking about those "crazy Victorians." The weed list from Monticello, reflecting the twenty worst weeds today, shows only three as being native. Lists of invasive plant varieties are available through county extension offices, or you can contact your local master gardener group.

A Legacy of the Landscape

Moving on to pests. Again, I will reference the Monticello lists, only this time there is a difference: the bulk of pests were native to this country. The most common ones seemed to be borers, beetles, cutworms, aphids and many of the same ones we combat today. Of course, like the weed, most controls were of a biological nature, like manual removal, crop rotation and plowing up the field and starting over. There were some chemicals used—lime, sulfur and tobacco dust, among several others. Before the eighteenth century, there were no serious pest or fungal problems, but once imported plants started being introduced, those numbers grew. With the farming techniques used, the imported pest population enlarged due to a lack of natural predators.

Pests that are a problem today include ticks and mosquitoes, although mosquitoes were remarked upon during the Lewis and Clark expedition in 1805: "Our trio of pests still invade and obstruct us on all occasions, these are the Musquetoes eye knats and prickley pears, equal to any three curses that ever poor Egypt laiboured under."[129] The Japanese beetle has a preference for roses, grapes, cannas, Japanese maples and crape myrtles, among other plants. I've always noted that they seem to like plants that have a lot of red pigmentation, but this is a personal observation. This beetle entered the country at Riverside, New Jersey, to be exact, prior to 1912, through a shipment of irises. This was before import inspections were done. One of the most recent invaders is the Asian long-horned beetle, which entered America in the 1980s in wood-packing material from China. The controls put into place now require all wood-packing material from China be either chemically treated or kiln dried. New Jersey's policy to control infestation is to cut down, chip and burn all healthy host trees within one-eighth to one-quarter of a mile radius of the infestation site. At Monticello, the most common pest of today is the eastern white-tailed deer. They are also a problem in New Jersey, as their environment gets encroached upon. There are plants deer and rabbits don't like that can be used in the landscape Again, one can get this and additional information from the local extension service or master gardeners.

Now for the pestilence part. When I was training to become a master gardener, one of the speakers quipped about New Jersey and fungus, "perfect together," a take on the state slogan at the time. What was being referred to are our very humid and hot summers, two ingredients that make for a perfect recipe to grow all kinds of diseases, powdery mildew, black spot and anthracnose, to name a few. Fire blight, as mentioned previously, was a problem with imported European pear trees until we learned to graft the rootstocks onto the native quince plants. A similar thing happened with imported grapes. Because of the many diseases imported grapes seemed

Oak leaf scorch.

prone to, "hybridization began in the mid-1800s to cross the disease resistance and winter hardiness of the native American species with the subtle flavor of vinifera (referring to the 'Old World' European grapes)."[130] Currently in New Jersey, we have a disease infecting the red, pin and scarlet oak trees called bacterial leaf scorch. It can also spread to other trees, like sycamore and elm. It is caused by a bacteria and spread by insects that feed on the xylem, the woody part of a stem used for transporting water and nutrients to the leaves. There is no known control at this time, and no one is sure how it started. It's kind of the Dutch elm disease of oaks right now.

A Legacy of the Landscape

Peter Hatch describes the problem:

> *Again the surprisingly large proportion of native versus introduced diseases suggests how North America is armed defensively with native pathogens to ward off the introduction of exotic horticultural fruits, ornamentals, and vegetables.*[131]

I will leave you with the following quote from Thomas Jefferson, so similar to the philosophy of gardening I find so fascinating and try to follow: "Such a variety of subjects, some one always coming to perfection, the failure of one thing repaired by the success of another, & instead of one harvest, a continued one thro' the year."[132]

The Future of Gardening in
New Jersey...and in Mount Holly

Recently, I was visiting Alexandria, Virginia. Standing in one of the shops looking at the selection of planters, I overheard two ladies talking. They were speaking loudly (I don't usually eavesdrop on people) about the garden plants they had recently started. None of the plants were anything complicated, but it was their first time, when the first tomato or green bean, is a really big deal. Such a sense of accomplishment comes with that feeling. With the prices of food escalating, it's not a bad idea to have a tomato or two hanging out in a pot on the patio.

In 2007, Americans spent $34 billion on their yards, according to *Newsweek*, with landscaping taking up nearly 47 percent of the total. Gardening is quickly becoming one of the fastest-growing hobbies out there. Now, because of problems with all the packaged produce, producing your own might be a good alternative. A lot more people are shopping at the local farmer's market now, looking for the fresh, organic fruits and vegetables. There's a lot more interest in the heirloom varieties, which seem to have more flavor than the normal store-bought items.

New Jersey has a Green Acre Program that sets up open spaces so people will have a system of connected open spaces to use as for recreational purposes. Burlington County is the home of several recreational parks provided by this program, which started in 1961. Movements to save farmland are becoming the norm across the country now. There's now a farmland preservation program in New Jersey.

As everyone is aware, we have to be concerned with our natural resources. One of them, about which every gardener is concerned, is water. Several areas of the country are now coming out of drought, but one never knows when circumstances may change. The leaf of a plant is 80 percent water.

Boxwood at the library.

A Legacy of the Landscape

Water must be replaced constantly. The pores of a leaf are always partially open. A plant needs seventeen times more water than a human does. Cacti and succulents are the only plants that carry their own water supply. Watering is a skill we must all learn when working with gardens, maintaining the balance of one's garden in relation to the larger environment. The need to conserve has also become a part of this skill set as well.

Mount Holly will never return to its mostly agricultural roots. We still have lots of lovely gardens in town that people can view on the Hidden Gardens Garden Tour we started in 2006. Can you believe there wasn't any garden tour prior to this? There is talk of starting a community garden once the correct space is found. Another Mount cleanup project is in the works. Last year, we had a mural painted along a pedestrian walkway called Cross Creek Alley. It is now time to get that garden started. Additionally, there are all the other public gardens that have been started and which need regular maintenance. The Mount Holly Garden Club is still around and doing well. Five years ago we added a Master Gardener program, which is also growing. Two of our local schools have some type of horticultural programs. Heck, I

Perennial flax, a Lewis and Clark discovery, growing in a backyard on the tour.

Fountain Square. *Courtesy of Larry Tigar.*

even found a Future Farmers of America chapter at one of them, although I'm not sure where my jacket is anymore.

There are several other gardens in the area about which I didn't get to write. There's the one at Smithville Mansion, owned by local industrialist H.B. Smith. Joseph Bonaparte, Napoleon's big brother, had an estate in a nearby town. I didn't get to mention Dr. James Still, the African American doctor of the Pines. His son lived in town, also practicing as a doctor. Of course, the gardens belonging to the common people, the laborers, many of which have been forgotten, still need some additional work.

I want to leave you with this little foreword, even though I am using it at the end, that Mike Eck at the Mount Holly Library sent to me when I was in a panic trying to get everything finished.

Many a time, I would arrive for work in the morning at the historic home
of the library, the Langstaff Mansion, and find her car parked in the lot

A Legacy of the Landscape

The Levis mural in Cross Creek Alley. *Courtesy of Lynn Lemyre.*

and know that she was somewhere about the library grounds with her snips, trimming boxwood, or weeding. I enjoyed ordering books, because I enjoyed them myself: using interlibrary loan, to order these obscure, 19th century, illustrated gardening books from libraries all over the country. We would discuss these and other important issues, like replacing the diseased centerpiece of the libraries' front landscaping with a Franklin Tree, or the latest journey to some historic garden in Virginia. All the more reason I look forward to seeing what she has to say about historic gardens: a subject that she cultivates with care.

I hope you have enjoyed this brief summary of some of Mount Holly's horticultural treasures. If you're ever in the area, there is a strong possibility, as Mike said, that I'll be at the library hanging out with one of my best friends, the boxwood.

Notes

GARDENS OF SURVIVAL

1. Jon E. Lewis, *The Mammoth Book of Native Americans* (New York: Carroll & Graf Publishers, 2004), 7.
2. Native Tech, "Planting a Three Sisters Garden," http://www.nativetech.org/cornhusk/threesisters.html.
3. Leah Blackman, *Leah Blackman's Old Times and Other Writings* (Tuckerton, NJ: Tuckerton Historical Society, 2000), 20.
4. Judith Sumner, *American Household Botany* (Portland, OR: Timber Press, 2004), 163.
5. Blackman, *Old Times*, 23.
6. Ibid., 27.
7. Bernard McMahon, *The American Gardener's Calendar* (Charlottesville, VA: The Thomas Jefferson Memorial Foundation, 1806; reprint 2005), 100.
8. Blackman, *Old Times*, 20.
9. McMahon, *American Gardener's Calendar*, 182.
10. Ibid., 190.
11. Pehr Kalm, *Travels into North America*, vol. 2 (London: T. Lowndes, 1773), 89.
12. Kalm, *Travels into North America*, vol. 1, 133.
13. McMahon, *American Gardener's Calendar*, 105.
14. Blackman, *Old Times*, 23.
15. Alice Morse Earle, *Old Time Gardens* (Lebanon, NH: First University Press of New England, 1901; reprint 2005), 196.
16. Blackman, *Old Times*, 20.

17. Earle, *Old Time Gardens*, 202.
18. Ibid., 204.
19. Peter J. Hatch, *The Fruit and Fruit Trees of Monticello* (Charlottesville: University of Virginia Press, 1998), 128.
20. Kalm, *Travels into North America*, vol. 1, 99.
21. Peter J. Hatch, "We abound in the Luxury of the Peach," *Twinleaf Journal* (January 1998), www.twinleaf.org/articles/peach.html.
22. Blackman, *Old Times*, 21.
23. Ibid.

LET'S GET STARTED

24. National Register of Historic Places Inventory, Nomination Form, Continuation Sheet 12, February 20, 1973.
25. Henry Shinn, *The History of Mount Holly* (Pemberton, NJ: Burlington County College, 1998), 6.
26. Dr. Zachariah Read, *Read's History of Mount Holly* (N.p., 1859), 11.
27. Ibid., 109.
28. Ibid.
29. Ibid., 110.

JOHN WOOLMAN'S GARDEN

30. John T. Faris, *Old Gardens In and About Philadelphia* (Indianapolis, IN: The Bobbs-Merrill Company, 1932), 231.
31. Ibid., 229.
32. George DeCou, *Historical Sketches of Mount Holly and Vicinity* (Mount Holly, NJ: Mount Holly Herald., 1936), 3.
33. Ibid.
34. Barbara Wells Sarudy, *Gardens and Gardening in the Chesapeake, 1700–1815* (Baltimore: The John Hopkins University Press, 1998), 114.
35. Faris, *Old Gardens*, 231.
36. Ibid., 232.
37. DeCou, *Historical Sketches*, 9.
38. Faris, *Old Gardens*, 237.

Timbuctoo

39. Rudy J. Favretti, "'Sprung From the Earth': the Layout of the Common Garden," in *Cultivating History Exploring Horticultural Practices of the Southern Gardener*, Proceedings of the Thirteenth Conference on Restoring Southern Gardens and Landscapes (Winston-Salem, NC: September 27–29, 2001), 38.
40. Patricia A. Gibbs, "Little Spots Allow'd Them: Eighteenth Century Slave Gardens and Poultry Yards," in *Cultivating History Exploring Horticultural Practices of the Southern Gardener*, Proceedings of the Thirteenth Conference on Restoring Southern Gardens and Landscapes (Winston-Salem, NC: September 27–29, 2001), 60.

America's First Millionaire

41. George Wilson, *Stephen Girard, the Life and Times of America's First Tycoon* (Conshohocken, PA: Combined Books, Inc., 1995), 372.
42. USHistory.org, s.v. "Stephen Girard," Independence Hall Association, http://www.ushistory.org/people/girard.htm.
43. Wilson, *Stephen Girard*, 94–95.
44. Rudy and Joy Favretti, *For Every House a Garden* (Lebanon, NH: University Press of New England, 1990), 30.
45. Thomas J. DiFilippo, *Stephen Girard, the Man, his College and Estate* (Online, 1999), http://www.girardweb.com/girard/welcome.htm.

Clover Hill/Ashurst Mansion

46. Shinn, *History of Mount Holly*, 127.
47. "Clover Hill Relic's Romance," newspaper article, Burlington County Historical Society.
48. Read, *Read's History*, 75.
49. John Bowie Associates, "Condition Assessment and Recommendation Report Mount Holly Library–Langstaff Mansion," November 12, 2002, 3.
50. Shinn, *History of Mount Holly*, 129.
51. Read, *Read's History*, 109.
52. Mary L. Smith, "The Ashurst Mansion at Clover Hill and the Underground Railroad," *Interesting Known Facts About Historical Mount Holly*, 1.

53. Ibid., 3.
54. Henry C. Shinn, "Clover Hill History Shows Panorama of Mount Holly," *Mount Holly Herald*, September 15, 1955.

LANGLELAND

55. Oliver Wendell Holmes, *Elsie Venner* (New York: Houghton-Mifflin, 1891).
56. "Local Affairs, Early Settlements in Springfield," *New Jersey Mirror*, February 9, 1881, Burlington County Library Systems, http://index. burlco.lib.nj.us/Mirror/njmirror.phtml.
57. Read, *Read's History*, 91.
58. Advertisement, "At a Special Term of the Court of Chancery," *New Jersey Mirror*, June 2, 1819, Burlington County Library Systems, http:// index.burlco.lib.nj.us/Mirror/njmirror.phtml.
59. Shinn, *History of Mount Holly*, 96.
60. Read, *Read's History*, 86.
61. McMahon, *American Gardener's Calendar*, 68.
62. Patrick Taylor, *Planting in Patterns* (New York: Harper & Row, 1989), 32.
63. McMahon, *American Gardener's Calendar*, 55.
64. John Bowie Associates, "Condition Assessment," 3.
65. Ibid., 6.
66. Ibid., 2.

THE CHINA–MOUNT HOLLY CONNECTION

67. Peter Coats, *The Gardens of Buckingham Palace* (London: Michael Joseph Ltd., 1978), 52–3.
68. John Rogers Haddad, *The Romance of China*, chap. 4, "China in Miniature: Nathan Dunn's Chinese Museum," http://www.gutenberg-e.org/haj01/haj05.html, 2.
69. Ibid.
70. David Cody, "Alexander Pope's Twickenham," The Victorian Web, http:// www.usp.nus.edu.sg/victorian/previctorian/pope/twickenham.
71. Haddad, *Romance of China*, 11.
72. Constance Greiff, "John Notman, Architect," The Athenaeum of Philadelphia, 1979, 61.

73. Leah Blackman, *History of Little Egg Harbor Township, Burlington County, NJ* (Trenton, NJ: Trenton Publishing Company, 1963), 282–83.

74. C.M. Havey, ed., *The Magazine of Horticulture, Botany, and all Useful Discoveries and Improvements in Rural Affairs*, vol. IX (Boston: Hovery & Co., 1843), 32.

RIVERSIDE AND THE BISHOP

75. John Howard Braun, *The Twentieth Century Biographical Dictionary of Notable Americans* (U.S. Biographical Society, 1904), 338.

76. Andrew Jackson Downing, *A Treatise on the Theory and Practice of Landscape Gardening* (Washington: Dumbarton Oaks, 1991), 118.

77. "Exploring Charms of the Delaware River," *New York Times*, February 1, 1920.

THE CEMETERY AS A GARDEN

78. "Local Facts and Fancies," *Mount Holly Mirror*, May 31, 1860, 2; Burlington County Library System, http://index.burlco.lib.nj.us/Mirror/njmirror.phtml, 35.

79. Andrew Jackson Downing, *Rural Essays* (New York: Leavitt & Allen, 1857), 154.

80. Downing, *Rural Essays*, 154–55.

81. Downing, *Treatise on the Theory*, 69.

82. Downing, *Rural Essays*, 157.

83. Daniel Bowen, *A History of Philadelphia: With Notice of Villages in the Vicinity* (Boston: Harvard University, 1839), 171.

84. Read, *Read's History*, 76–77.

85. Elizabeth M. Perinchief, *History of Cemeteries in Burlington County, N.J. 1687–1975* (Mount Holly, NJ: E.M. Perinchief, 1978).

86. Read, *Read's History*, 110–11.

87. "Local Facts and Fancies," 35.

88. *Joseph C. Cowgill Scrapbook*, Mount Holly Historical Society Collection. Joseph Cowgill collected a vast array of Mount Holly memorabilia from 1840 to 1900. Much of what is known about Mount Holly from this time period is because of his scrapbook.

89. Ibid.

THE OTHERS

90. Henry C. Shinn, "Clover Hill Estate Provides Rich Historical Interest," *Mount Holly Herald*, September 15, 1955.
91. Ibid.
92. Read, *Read's History*, 109.
93. Ibid.
94. Ibid.
95. Federal Writer 7, Projects of the Works Progress Administration for the State of New Jersey, *New Jersey, A Guide to Its Present and Past* (New York, The Viking Press, 1939), 297.
96. Ibid.
97. Joel T. Fry, "Re: Bartram Oak," e-mail to author, June 23, 2006.
98. Shinn, *History of Mount Holly*, 110.
99. William Bispham, *Memoranda Concerning the Family of Bispham in Great Britain and the United States of America* (Privately published, 1890), 240.
100. Read, *Read's History*, 34.
101. Shinn. *History of Mount Holly*, 111.
102. Bispham, *Memoranda*, 241.
103. Ibid.
104. "Local Facts and Fancies/Notice of Mount Holly, by a Visitor," *New Jersey Mirror*, July 22, 1858, Burlington County Library Services.
105. Cowgill, *Scrapbook*.
106. Ibid.
107. Ibid.
108. Read, *Read's History*, 86.
109. Henry C. Shinn, "Bispham Family Merits High Place in Mount Holly History," *Mount Holly Herald*, October 21, 1954.
110. N. Webster and C. Dillon, *Margaret Morris, Burlington-N.J. 1804 Gardening Memorandum*, (Chillicothe, IL: The American Botanist, 1996).

A DESTINATION LOCATION

111. Farris, *Old Gardens*, 234.
112. The Last Will and Testament of Nathan Dunn, dated July 13, 1841, in possession of Burlington County Lyceum of Natural Sciences and History, Mount Holly Library.
113. "Mrs. J.D. Johnson Died This Morning; Stricken Week Ago," *New Jersey Mirror*, January 29, 1936, 1.

114. Father David Adams, "Re: Nathan Dunn's gardens," e-mail to author, June 29, 2005.

115. Cowgill, *Scrapbook*, May 1887.

116. Notice, *New Jersey Mirror*, March 6, 1918, http://www.burlco.lib.nj.us/genealohy/newjerseymirror/njmirror.phtml.

117. Faris, *Old Gardens*, 236–37.

Snippets

118. Cowgill, *Scrapbook*, 1886.

119. Decou, *Historical Sketches*, 5.

120. Mount Holly Historical Society, *Historic Mount Holly, New Jersey* (Mount Holly, NJ: 1973), 17.

121. Faris, *Old Gardens*, 235.

122. Ibid., 236.

123. Ibid., 235.

124. Ibid., 236.

125. Cowgill, *Scrapbook*.

126. Ibid.

Pests and Pestilence

127. McMahon, *American Gardener's Calendar*, 380.

128. Peter Hatch, "Garden Weeds in the Age of Jefferson," *Twinleaf*, 2006, www.twinleaf.org/articles/index.html.

129. Gary Moulton, *The Lewis and Clark Journals* (Lincoln: Board of Regents of the University of Nebraska, 2003), 156.

130. "Winemaking," Explore New Jersey Wine Country, www.newjerseywines.com.

131. Peter Hatch, "Ecological Imperialism? Southern Garden Pests and Pesticides, 1700–1832," *Cultivating History Exploring Horticultural Practices of the Southern Gardener*, Proceedings of the Thirteenth Conference on Restoring Southern Gardens and Landscapes (Winston-Salem, NC: September 27–29, 2001), 97.

132. John Kaminski, *Citizen Jefferson, The Wit and Wisdom of an American Sage* (Madison, WI: Madison House Publishers, Inc.), 42.

About the Author

Alicia McShulkis is a Mount Holly resident and lives here with her husband and three children. She works as the events coordinator for Main Street Mount Holly, where she started as a volunteer. She has written and lectured on historic gardening for the Burlington County Master Gardeners, as well as Main Street Mount Holly. As a chairperson for the design comittee, Alicia oversaw improvements to the Cross Creek Alley and earned Main Street Mount Holly and the Mount Holly Historical Society a Suburban Greening Award from the Pennsylvania Horticultural Society for her work at Fountain Square. In 2006, Alicia was given a proclamation by Mount Holly Township for her volunteer work in the community. When not working on Main Street Mount Holly events, Alicia works as a volunteer gardener with Burlington County Master Gardeners and at the Mount Holly Library.

Visit us at
www.historypress.net